# Small Interiors

LINKS

Edition 2008

Author: Dimitris Kottas
Publisher: Carles Broto
Graphic designer & production: Oriol Vallès
Text: Contributed by the architects, edited by William George and Marta Rojals

© Carles Broto i Comerma
Jonqueres, 10, 1-5
08003 Barcelona, Spain
Tel.: +34 93 301 21 99
Fax: +34 93 301 00 21
E-mail: info@linksbooks.net
www.linksbooks.net

# Small Interiors

LINKS

# index

# introduction

Creation depends on the space and the possibilities that it affords. Therefore, architectural work in small spaces is often a challenge in which one must achieve the seemingly impossible: to turn a small space into a comfortable dwelling in which the lack of living space is not perceived. Great architectural works are not necessarily those that are measured by the number of square meters.

The aim of this book is to show those designs that stand out for their skill in creating stimulating environments in small spaces. This is a complicated task that is not limited to removing partitions, building mezzanines and incorporating specific furniture for the needs of the space. A skillful use of a small space requires far more: one must also think of the requirements and the comfort of the clients, and devise an aesthetic design in which the architecture can adapt to the restrictions of a limited floor area.

These works show the imaginative force of the designs in which small premises can be transformed into comfortable dwellings, regardless of their original use or location.

The designs include apartments created after the division of a large flat, small single-family dwellings in the country and fantasy terrace dwellings. They are complemented by plans and explanations of the architectural work carried out in each scheme, all of which is proof positive that creative design does not depend on the available floor space.

# Christian Pottgiesser

## 24, Rue Buisson Saint Louis

*Photographs: Luc Boegly*

**Paris, France**

This small plot of some thirty-plus square meters is surrounded on three and a half sides by the blind walls of neighboring buildings, a condition which limited the possibilities for achieving natural lighting. On the remaining side, an imposing five-story building made for very undesirable views.

The program called for a neutral central space free from technical interferences and defined by three key elements.

First, a wide glass strip demarcates the outer edges, diffusing and interpreting the natural and artificial sources of light.

A second, thicker 'strip' encasing the living space duplicates the lateral blind walls. Built into or growing from this encasement are a number of the components that are required in habitable spaces, such as alcoves set aside for eating, resting, sleeping, and so forth, as well as modules with no a priori function.

Finally, upstairs is a folded, reinforced concrete surface that has been molded to the limits allowed by the adjacent buildings, while also deflecting the least desirable views.

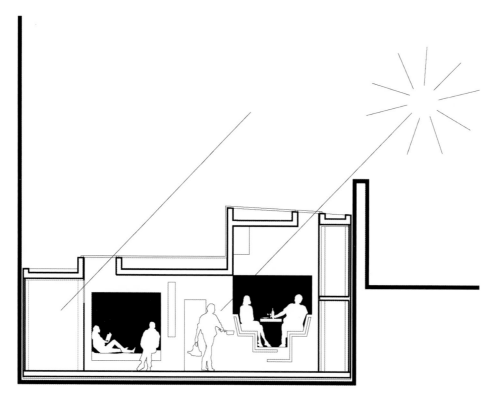

Section

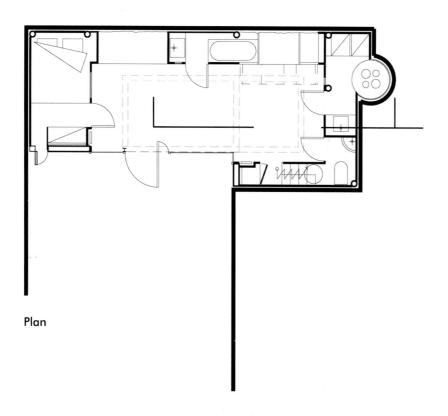

Plan

# Marc (Michele Bonino & Subhash Mukerjee) with Federica Patti, Martina Tabò

www.studiomarc.eu

## House in Torino

Photographs: Beppe Giardino

Turin, Italy

A couple in their thirties bought an elegant corner apartment in a 19th century building in the center of Turin.

The apartment was very spacious and had interesting views towards a large gardened boulevard.

The main problem of the remodeling that Coex were asked to design was the big, dark entrance: the clients loved its finely worked continuous terrazzo floor and of course wanted to make it a pleasing and functional space. On the other hand it had no windows and received no natural light. Coex decided to make that space the core and engine of the whole flat.

The entrance is invaded by a massive volume containing "dark functions" - a shower and some storage space. To preserve the integrity of the floor, the volume "flies" one meter above and the contained functions are only accessible from the back. The volume also serves as a big lamp for the entrance providing direct illumination throughout this level. To take advantage of the views and to enhance the apartment's sense of spaciousness, the two requested bathrooms are compressed behind the volume.

In accordance with the clients' brief, the other rooms have been left almost undesigned, thus emphasizing the contrast between the dark and dense private areas and the light-filled, airy living spaces.

Central to the design is this masonry volume cantilevered out over the entrance and containing the main bedroom's walk-in closet and an open cloakroom in one corner. Here, the existing terrazzo floor has been preserved in its entirety.

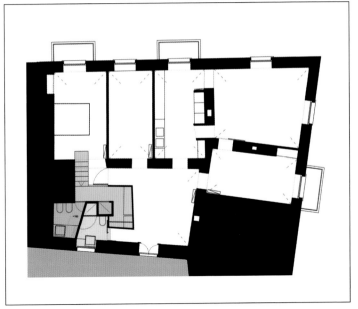

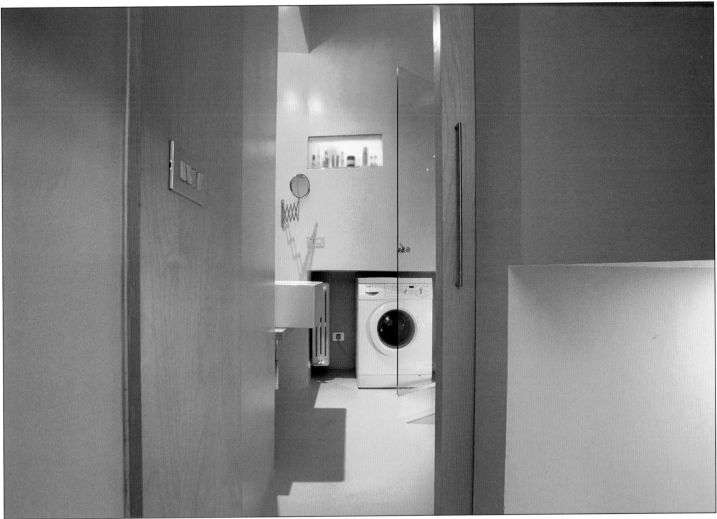

The kitchen is well-communicated with the living/dining area, although visually separated by a fixed unit housing kitchen equipment and appliances. All of the flooring in this area is the apartment's original oak parquet.

The stairs to the bathroom are paved in dark Brazilian ferrous slate, with the warm beech plywood flooring of the master bedroom set in gentle counterpoint.

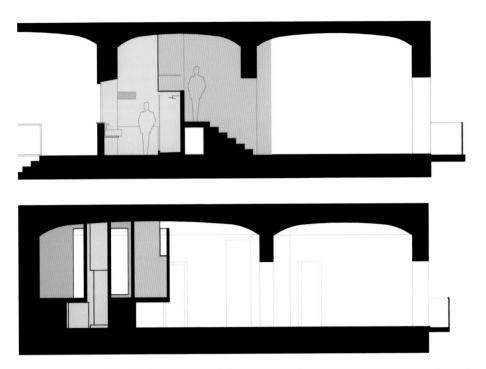

The raised bathroom and walk-in closet sit adjacent to the master bedroom. This volume, which sits one meter above the rest of the apartment in the corner of the plan, is an ingenious reworking of limited space.

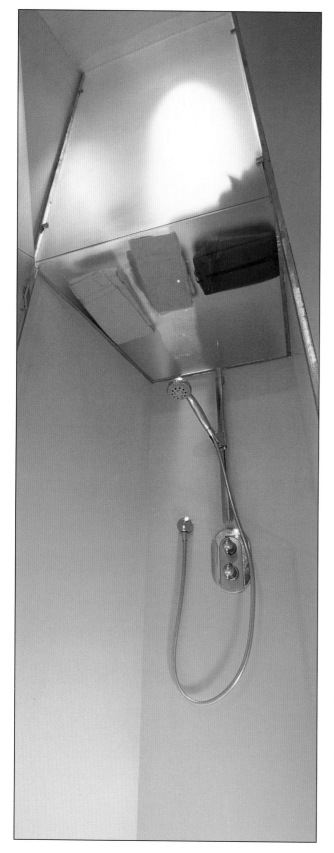

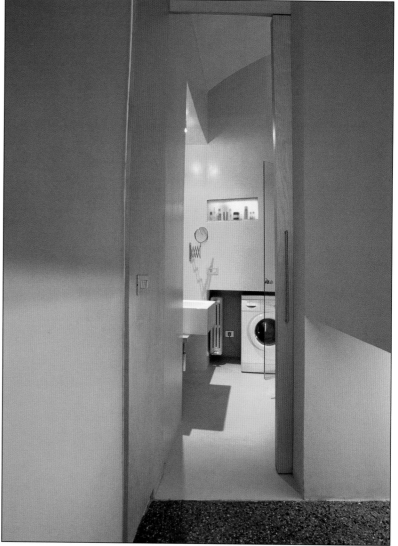

# Ian Hay

## Hay Apartment

photographs:
*Richard Glover*

London, UK

Housed in two rooms on the first floor of a modest Georgian terrace off Tottenham Court Road, and occupying only 320 sqft, this apartment was designed around the premise that Hay wanted a spacious house in a very small space. He refused to make the compromises usual in studio-sized flats, such as having a shower instead of a bath, or putting the kitchen in the living room. Instead, he began by calculating the minimum space required to cook, or for a double bed, then looked at ways in which these functions could be combined within the limited space.

The flat may have everything, but it is not always where you would expect to find it. The bathroom, for instance, is on a platform above the bed, and from the bath, there is a choice of views: you can open up a hatch to watch a small TV beside the bed, or see through the kitchen into the front room. The front room itself doubles as a work pace, with a large table that folds down from the wall so that Hay can run his practice from home.

One key to the success of this very tight conversion is the play on transparency. Neither the bathroom nor the kitchen are treated as enclosed rooms, and surprising sightlines run through the flat, so that the claustrophobic feeling associated with tight, boxed-in spaces is avoided.

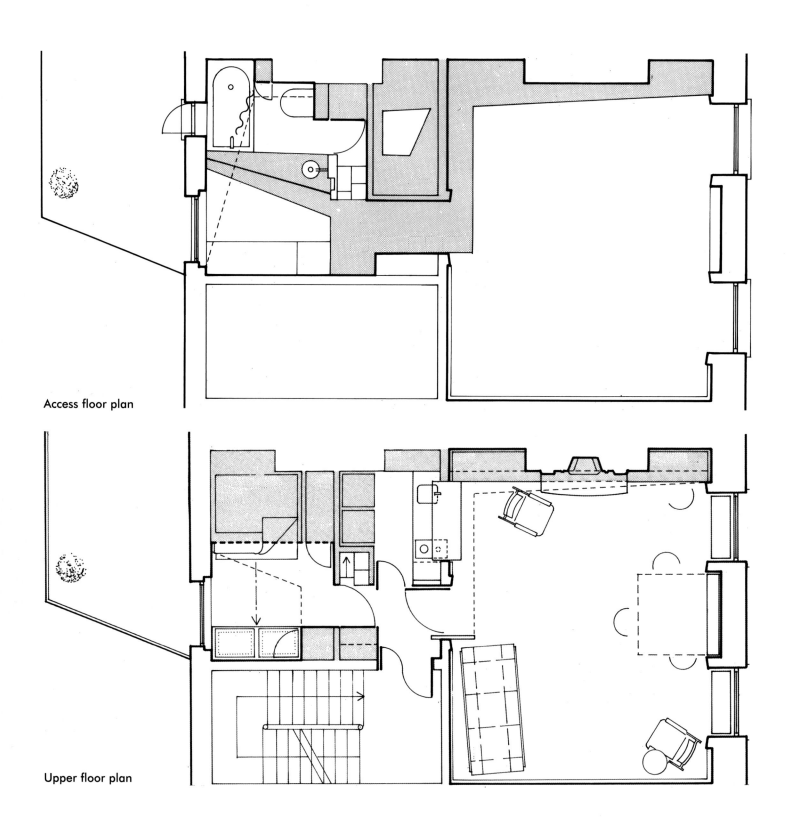

Access floor plan

Upper floor plan

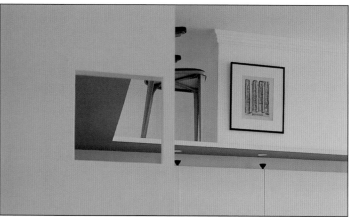

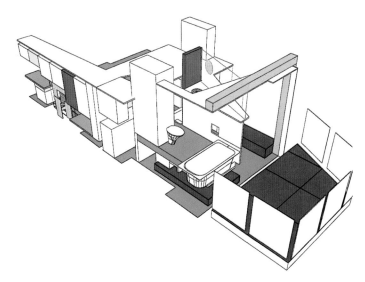

# i29 office for spatial design

## Heart of the home + Blossom

Photographs:
i29 office for spatial design

Dutch design company i29 are masters at maximising small spaces, creating award-winning solutions in answer to the problems of limited space. Here they outline two examples of what they describe as their leefmachines or 'living machines', their own particular brand of furniture/ interior design.

The first, known as the 'heart of the home', has transformed a compact apartment of 55sqm in Amsterdam into a luxurious home. In the centre of the apartment they designed a unit which comprises a bathroom, kitchen and storage space, all together as one object. The most important feature is that the unit is a compact box, a 'living machine', with a household around it. In this way optimal spatial experience is guaranteed. The designers' idea is that a piece of furniture like this should be custom built according to the needs of the clients, bearing in mind their way of life.

The design is minimalist and finely detailed. By integrating the different elements - the cupboards, bathroom and kitchen - it leaves the rest of the space in the apartment to be experienced as a whole. All fronts and doors have been made gripless to express the autonomy of the object. Materials and design have been carefully chosen to create a unique atmosphere. The rest of the furnishings are from Vitra, Moooi and Spectrum

This compact city apartment is divided into three zones: the front, which gives on to the street, is the kitchen, dining and socializing area; the middle area is for living and relaxing, while the back which gives on to the garden is the quiet sleeping and reading area. Although there are no walls or any dividing objects, these different areas are still very clearly defined thanks to the custom-built unit which organizes the rest of the space.

In another remarkable example of how to resolve the problem of restricted space, they have designed a unit, named Blossom, which contains a bed, toilet, shower and sink for a private home in Wassenaar in Holland. Everything about this volume is sleek and compact. Glass doors lead to the shower and toilet, both of which are finished in polyester. At the front of the unit a sink and mirror are integrated.

In a twenty-first century take on the four-poster bed a design of blossoming tree branches printed on voile surround the bed, giving the sensation of light and springtime the whole year round.

This project was presented at the VSK Baden in Holland trade fair in Utrecht. In addition i29 received an honourable mention for the interior design of this bed and bathroom at the Bathroom Design Awards 2006 in Holland which was awarded to them at the Jaarbeurs Utrecht trade fair and exhibition centre.

**HEART OF THE HOME**
Location:
Amsterdam,
The Netherlands
Total floor area: 55 sqm

**BLOSSOM**
Location:
Wassenaar,
The Netherlands
Total floor area:
35 sqm

## Heart of the home

## Blossom

# Heart of the home

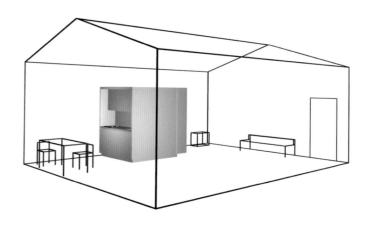

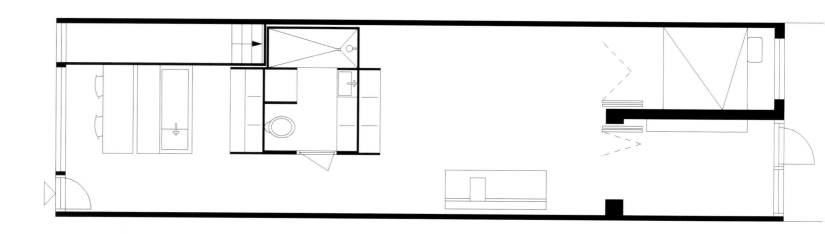

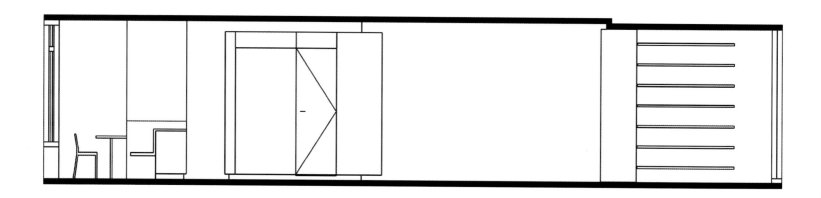

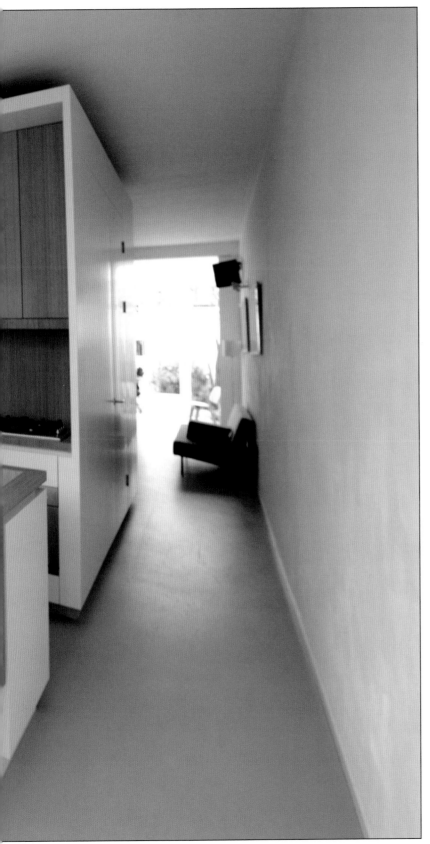

# Blossom

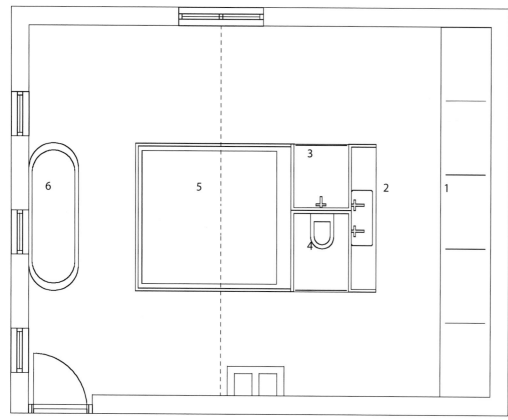

1. Wardrobe
2. Washing stand
3. Shower
4. Toliet
5. Bed
6. Bath

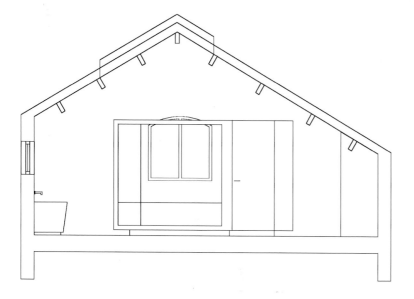

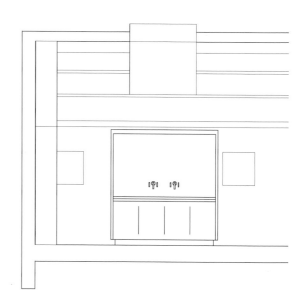

48

# Bromley Caldari

## Emi's Apartment

*Photographs:*
*José Luis Hausmann*

New York, USA

The fact that this apartment is a second residence has defined some characteristics of its design. The client was a Japanese business woman who needed a place of her own to inhabit during her periods of work in New York. The program required that the living room and the bedroom be considered as main priorities, as these were going to be the spaces most used. The windows of the living room are of generous dimensions and there is an unusually long sofa in this space, designed to hold the maximum number of guests. Opposite this there is a false panel which contains the complete musical and video equipment, with Television and DVD.

The bedroom is reached through a sliding door which also communicates with the bathroom and the dresser.

The sofa, which was designed to specifications, has a wooden frame and is upholstered in grey velvet. The pillows are of Thai silk and the table in the center combines the glass top with a base of tinted steel.

The shelves, made of ash wood, allow for a maximum rational use of space within the bedroom. So as to conceal them whenever it is considered convenient, the architects have designed the silk curtains that give the sleeping area a more intimate ambiance.

Curved wall panels have been inserted into what was once a pre-dominantly rectilinear space, the end result being a much more fluid, organic ambience. The sofa, which was designed to specifications, has a wooden frame and is upholstered in grey velvet. The pillows are of Thai silk and the table in the center combines a glass top with tinted steel base.

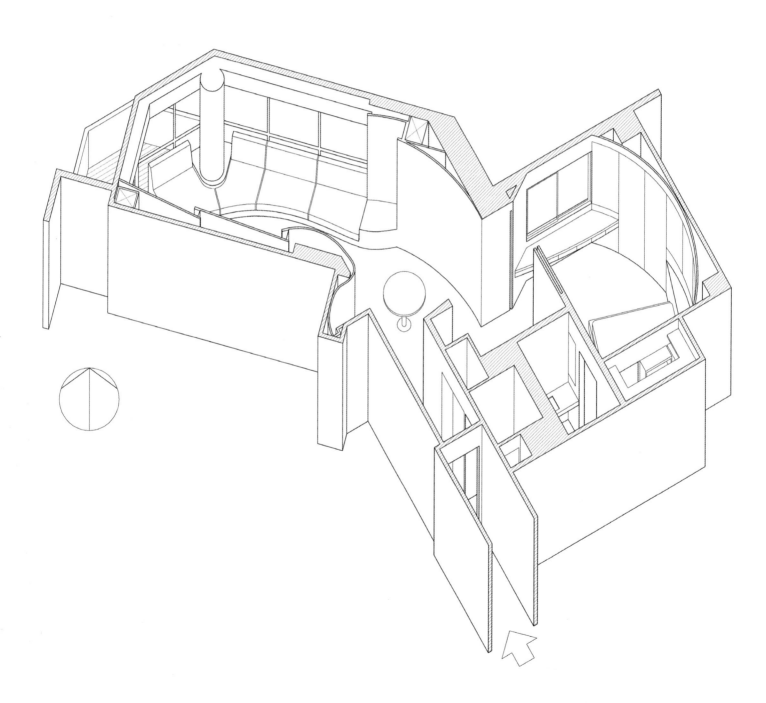

Floor plan

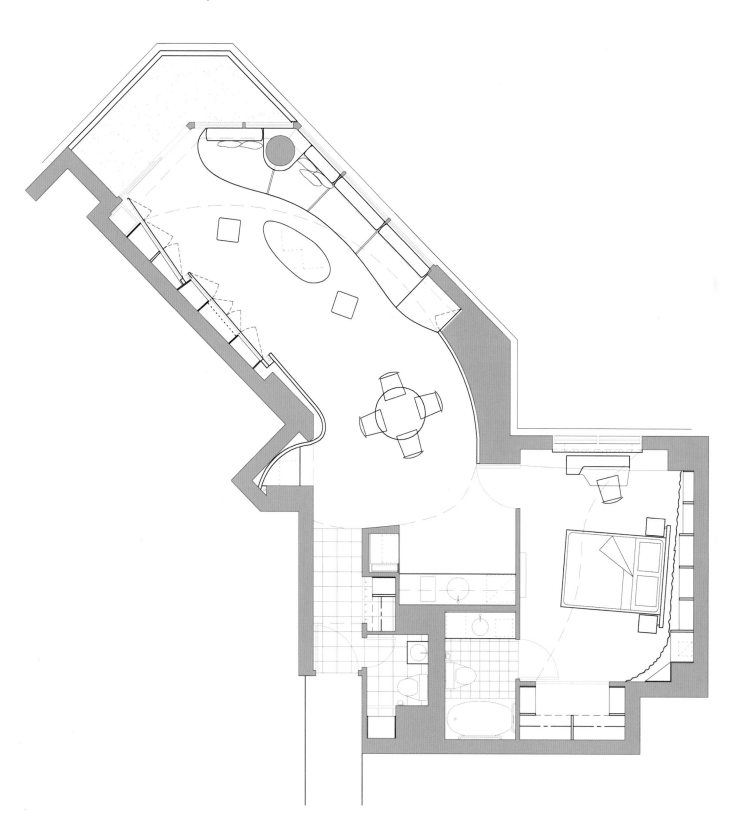

Rationality combined with luxury was the underlying theme for this residence which would be used only partially and, even then, for entertaining.

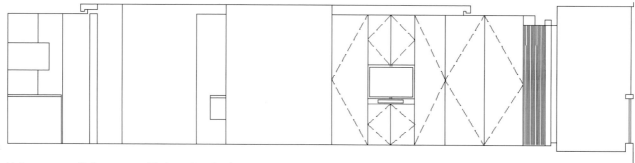

Living room, dining room, kitchen South elevation

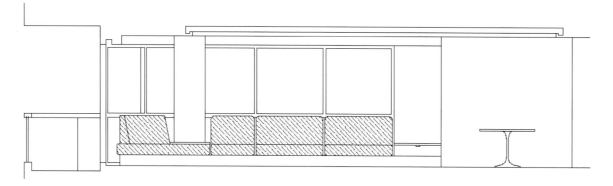

Living room, dining room, kitchen North elevation

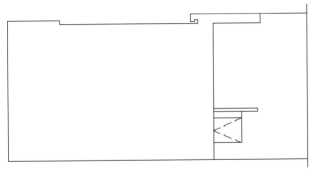

Entry / Tokonoma West elevation

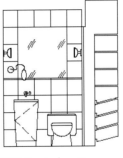

WC East elevation

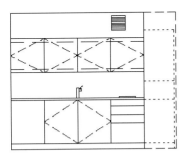

Kitchen elevation

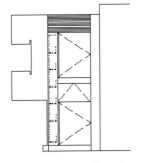

Kitchen / Pantry elevation

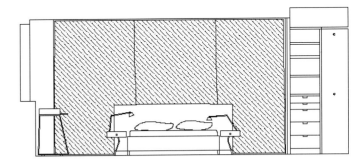

Bed room East elevation

# David Maturen

## Apartment Zaragoza David

Photographs: Jordi Miralles

**Zaragoza, Spain**

Carried out in 2001, the project called for the complete overhaul of an attic loft in a building dating from 1903. The design scheme was centered on the search for the diaphanous and homogenous in the spaces, while ensuring that natural light reached every corner of the apartment. The furnishings and wall hangings were meticulously chosen by the architects, giving the space as a whole a note of elegance and warmth.

The flooring on the lower level has been done in stone tiles measuring 60x80 centimeters. In the loft, where the second bedroom is housed, the floor is wood. Plexiglass and acid-finished glass were used for the partitions and windows. The stainless steel finishes are perfectly integrated into the minimalist design of the apartment.

The distribution of the furnishings and fixtures defines the divisions between the living room/dining room and the bedroom and kitchen. The bathroom is the only space that has been completely closed off. The element that ultimately defines the spaces is the pronounced slope of the roof.

A metal spiral staircase set discreetly alongside the entrance, as if it were just another fixture, provides access to the main loft. There is another loft above the kitchen which is accessed via a folding ladder.

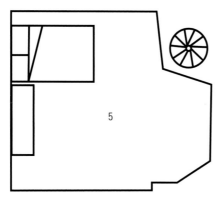

1. Hall
2. Bathroom
3. Kitchen
4. Living dining room
5. Bedroom
6. Closet

Upper floor plan

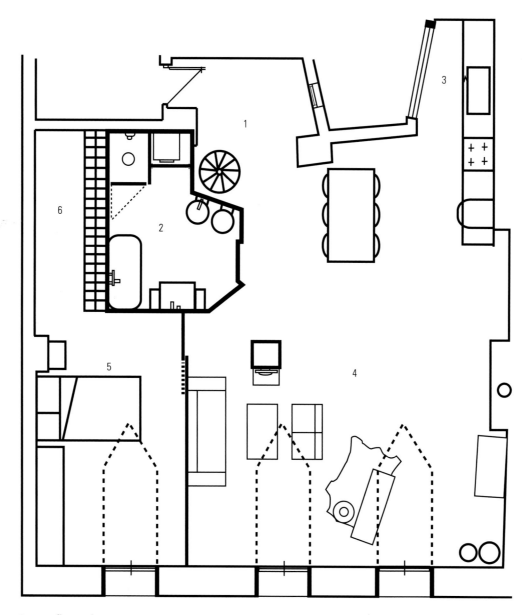

Lower floor plan

There are two separate lofts, each accessed via its own stair or ladder system. The secondary loft, set above the kitchen, features a folding ladder for easy access while a classic spiral staircase provides the elegant entry to the main loft.

# Claeson, Koivisto & Rune

## Apartment in Stockhlom

photographs:
Patrick Engquist

Stockhlom, Sweden

The task confronting this team of three architects was to create a comfortable, uncluttered living space in a very small area.

The apartment, located in the centre of Stockholm, has a total floor area of just 33.5 sqm, comprised basically of one open-plan room, with adjoining concrete-tiled terrace and blue mosaic-tiled bathroom, connected to the main room by a small opening with a sliding acid-etched window.

Despite its size, the apartment has all the necessary conveniences. Non-living space storage, dishwasher, refrigerator, freezer, microwave and so on are either built-in or concealed behind doors, resulting in a serene and minimalist aesthetic in which to conduct domestic life. Although the work of several designers has been used in the finished project, all the built-in furnishings were designed by the architects themselves.

The terrace furniture can easily be lifted inside for occasions demanding more seating space, and the futon bed doubles up as a sofa. All the lighting and two motorized Venetian blinds are controlled from one centrally placed panel. The Venetian blinds, when shut, hide both the windows and the work desk.

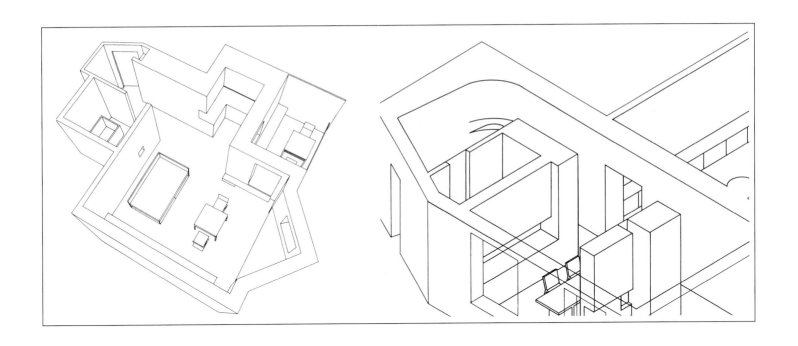

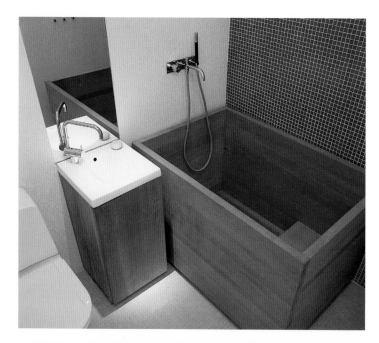

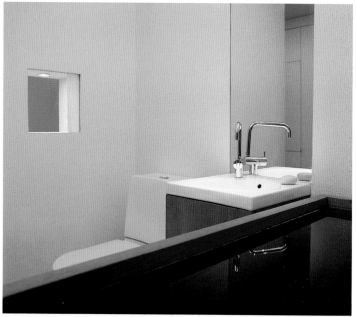

The dwelling is ordered around a small single room, but the architects have managed to give the apartment full visual and spatial opening.

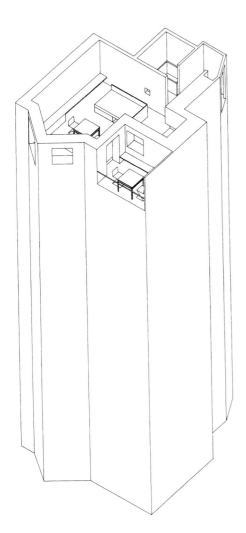

# Johanna Grawunder

## Beach House in Milan

Photographs: Santi Caleca

**Milan, Italy**

The design approach for the interior of this beach house was to look for the "essence" of the existing open space and respect it as much as possible.

This was achieved by painting the existing concrete structure matt black in order to highlight it, so that the structure itself became the most striking element of the loft. The emphasis was on creating an easy and elegant environment, using mainly inexpensive materials, and leaving different areas as open as possible while allowing the structure to define the space.

The few volumes in the space arose from the need for some private areas within this very strong cultural grid. In order to respect the mainly post and beam construction, the few walls that where required were designed to look like separate volumes, huddling under the structural grid.

Paint was used to define the space and create different effects, black for the structural grid, light blue for the ceiling, and different shades of green and gray for the volumes. The finishes and furniture were carefully chosen to create an environment where various levels of refinement could comfortably coexist - a few custom designed pieces mixed with other simple and inexpensive or industrial-style furniture.

The house consists of a master bedroom and bathroom, a simple kitchen and an open plan living area. Sliding doors separate the bedroom from the main room, so that it can be open to the rest of the house. The emphasis is on maximum flexibility of use and movement through the space.

Interior elevation

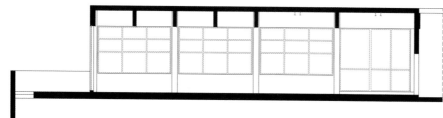

The living room is the main open loft-like space and has only basic furniture, mostly out of the way, so that there is maximum flexibility. The simple black laminate kitchen opens up to the rest of the main room, with two steel carts which serve as storage and a preparation island.

# GCA & Associats

## House in Costa Brava

Photographs:
*Jose Luis Hausmann*

**Llafranch, Girona, Spain**

This project called for the overhaul of a single-family, two-story house in Llafranch. The layout of the home was unusual, with the upper floor reserved exclusively for the parents, and the ground floor divided into two separate apartments, one for each child.

The decision was made to adapt a space of some 755 sqft (70 sqm) to the needs of one person. The apartment is accessed directly from the garden, the first space on entering being a single open space bringing together the kitchen, dining room and living room all in one.

Separated by sliding doors in painted wood and translucent metal mesh is the main bedroom. These sliding doors grant a sense of intimacy and depth to this space.

The kitchen has been finished primarily in stainless steel, with the front panels of the cabinetry finished in textured blue paint. Just opposite the kitchen is a maple wood table with built-in drawers on casters (also in textured blue) that provide space for storing kitchen utensils. This table bridges the gap between the dining room and the rest of the dwelling.

The living room is set to one side of the kitchen. One of its walls features a built-in bench and maple wood shelves. The furniture consists of a couch and two armchairs, all upholstered in white. All auxiliary furniture pieces are movable and multi-use in order to create a sense of spaciousness and versatility.

On the other side of the kitchen is the bedroom. The headboard is also in maple wood and features a built-in cubby hole that also serves as a small shelf. A walk-in closet and a bathroom are accessed from one side of the bedroom.

One of the walls in the bathroom has been finished in stucco stained the same blue as in the kitchen. The bathroom sink unit is in teak, with a stainless steel basin. The tap is the Tara model by Dorn Bracht.

A small guest room with its own bathroom is set at the other end of the apartment.

All of the walls have been stuccoed in a stone color, while the carpentry displays natural tones, and the ceiling beams have been painted blue.

Foor plan

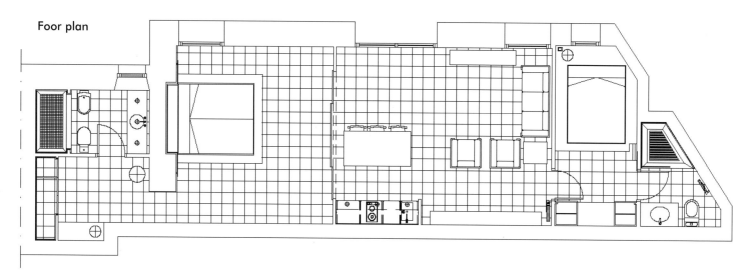

The living room is set to one side of the kitchen. One of its walls features a built-in bench and maple wood shelves. The furniture consists of a couch and two armchairs, all upholstered in white. All auxiliary furniture pieces are movable and multi-use in order to create a sense of spaciousness and versatility.

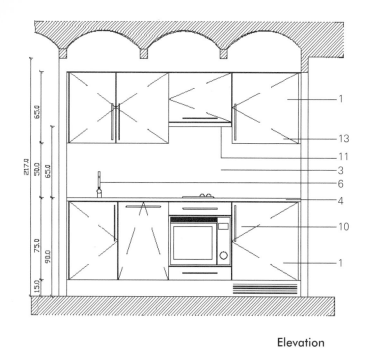

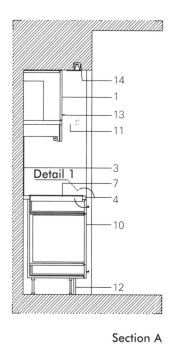

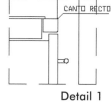

**Elevation**

**Section A**

Detail 1

**Section B**

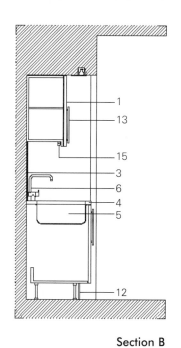

**Plan**

CANTO RECTO

**Detail 1**

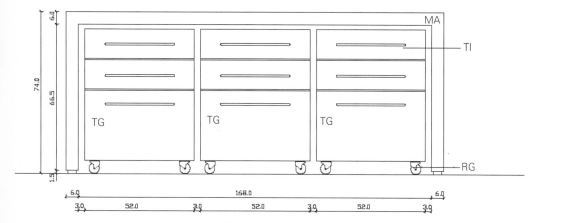

MA

TI

TG   TG   TG

RG

6.0   52.0   3.0   52.0   3.0   52.0   3.0

168.0

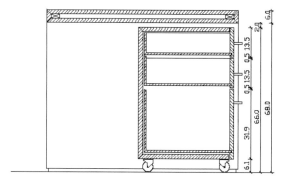

1. Cabinetry front panels in textured DM. Gray Ral anthracite
2. Sides in stainless steel
3. Apron of countertop in matte stainless steel
4. Countertop in matte stainless steel
5. Kitchen sink in stainless steel for stowing beneath countertop. Smeg mod BST 30, 11.8in X 17.7in (30 X 45cm)
6. Stainless steel kitchen tap, Vola series Model KV 1
7. Neff Modd vitrious China. Domino 139 with stainless steel frame
8. Built-in refrigerator, Liebherr Model KIU 1424
9. Built-in dishwasher, Bosch,    Model SPV 4503, 17.7in (45cm)
10. Microwave oven Neff Mod Mega 7869 in stainless steel
11. Telescopic extractor hood Smeg Mod. KSET60X + KITB60X
12. Stainless steel base
13. Stainless steel pull knobs by Didheya, Model 1131
14. Inlaid halogen spotlighting by Lumiance, Mod Instar 70, Cool 50, matte silver
15. Fluorescent tubes beneath overhead cup boards

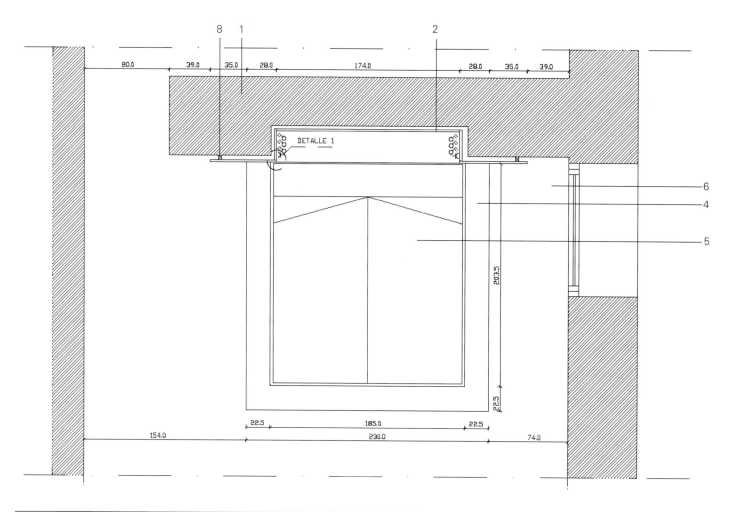

DETALLE 1

80.0  39.0  35.0  28.0  174.0  28.0  35.0  39.0

203.5

22.5

22.5  185.0  22.5

154.0  230.0  74.0

1. Maple wood paneling
2. Inlaid shelf lined in textured DM, color to be defined
3. Indirect lighting by Agabekov, Mod. Universal 1 Xenon
4. Maple wood platform
5. Mattress
6. Tufa flooring
7. Bticino fixtures, Light series
8. Fillets
9. Paint

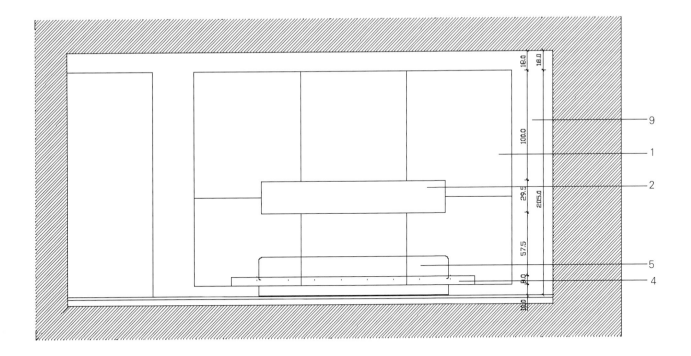

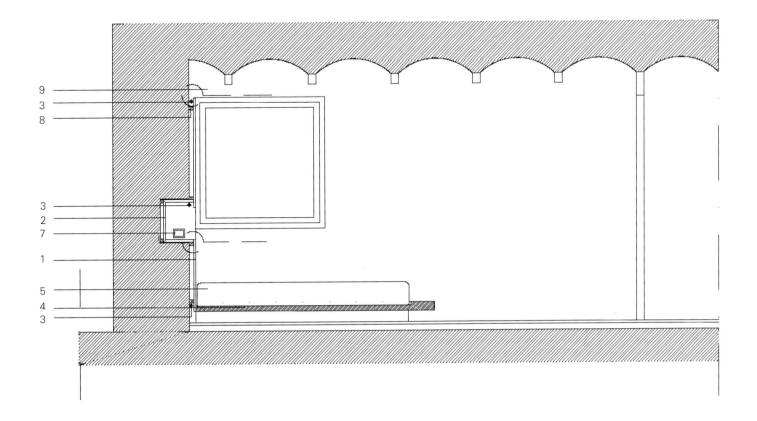

# Sergio Calatroni

## Gallery dwelling Uchida

Photographs:
Sergio Calatroni

**Milan, Italy**

The project consists in rehabilitating a 90 sqm space situated in the city of Milan, in order to adapt it and convert it into a gallery dwelling.

The gallery, in which works of art by the owner of the dwelling are exhibited, is on the first level. This floor are also houses the kitchen and a small bathroom, whereas the whole of the upper floor is taken up by the bedroom and the main bathroom. The lower floor communicates through large French windows with a terrace that provides the space with light.

The whole project is articulated by means of fixed and mobile walls.

The kitchen and the bathroom on the lower floor are separated from the gallery by means of a movable panel. The geometric finishes of this panel were made by combining white, black and reddish wood. The floor, a magnificent surface of cherry wood, brings unity to the dwelling.

A minimalist staircase of folded sheet leads to the upper floor where the bedroom is located. The two-toned sculptural element that divides the staircase and also performs the function of a banister was made in Greek-work sheet.

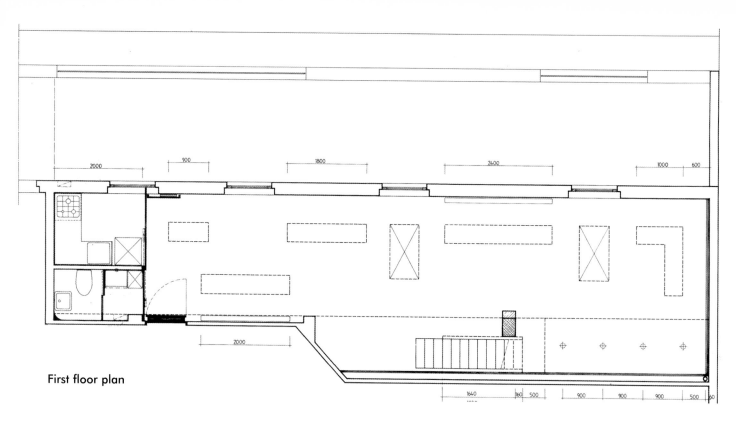

First floor plan

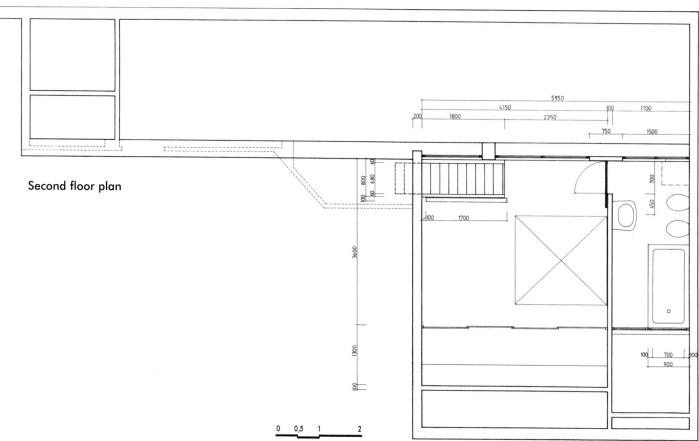

Second floor plan

0  0,5  1      2

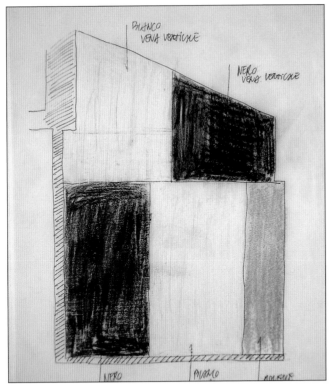

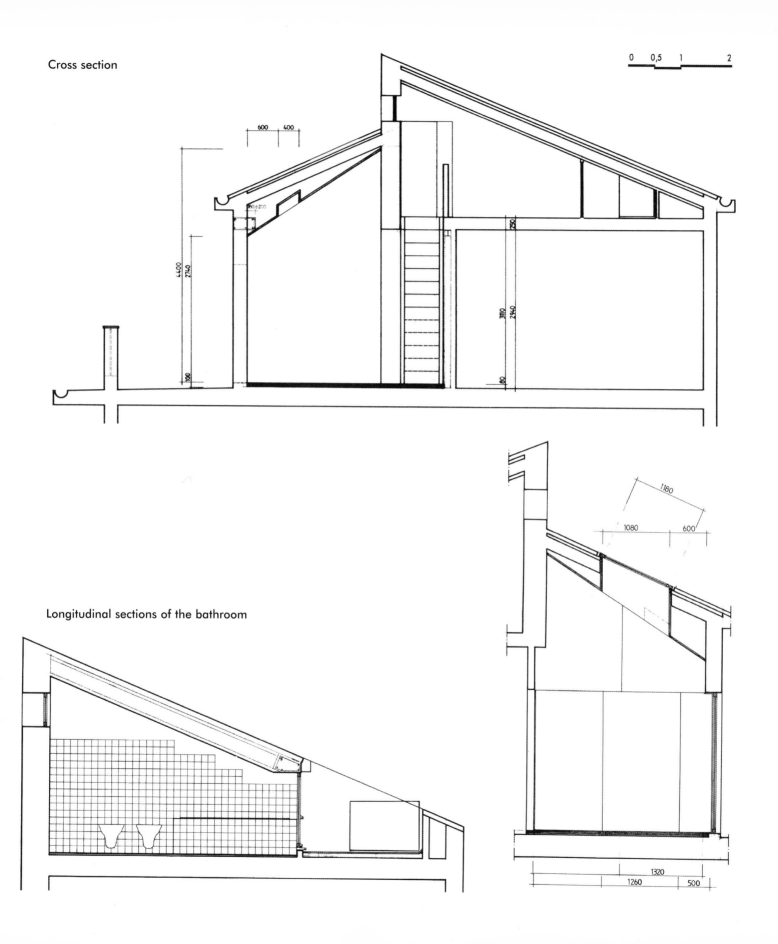

Cross section

Longitudinal sections of the bathroom

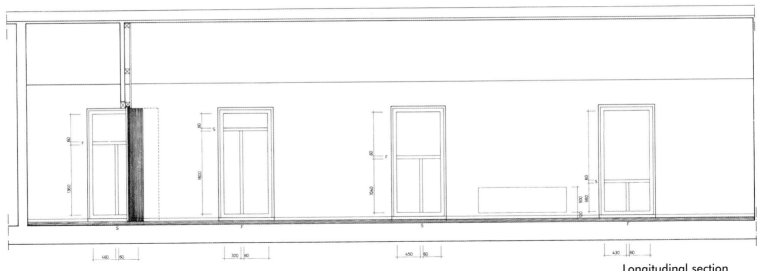

Longitudinal section

### Construction detail of the window

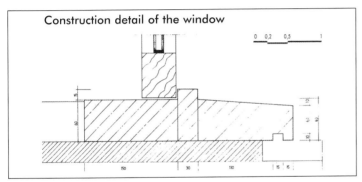

0  0,2   0,5        1

# Jean-Pierre Lévêque

## House in Rue Compans

*Photographs: Hervé Abbadie*

**Paris, France**

This building, an old laboratory built in the thirties, was transformed into an inhabitable space after twenty years. It is located in a complex fabric of plots, a kind of a residual space in the form of an isosceles triangle between two five-storey blocks.

For the rehabilitation of this small dwelling of 80 sqm, the brief was to optimise its habitability and to rediscover in the space a clear legibility and its initial constitution as a building suspended over a covered exterior.

The layout offered the possibility of creating a multi-purpose space defined by the exterior and interior elements. The ground floor was left completely open in order to allow the exterior, consisting of the covered courtyard, to be extended completely into the house. Inside this covered exterior, a differentiated structure containing the kitchen was inserted. This "box" is completely open within the continuous layout of the floor, walls and ceiling, thus giving the dwelling a distinguished appearance.

The exterior of this volume is secured by means of the lower part of the room, and by the pillar that supports it. The house is therefore suspended, with the areas that require greater domestic privacy, such as the bedrooms and the bathroom, at the top.

All the spaces were connected to each other by means of a wooden strip. This begins as the main envelope of the kitchen, becomes the staircase that gives access to the first floor and ends in a wide bookcase before leading to the bedrooms. This "Ariadne's thread", ensures maximum fluidity, multiplying all possible points of view on the area of the dining room and the kitchen in the ascent to the first level, in which all the dimensions of the space that one moves through are apparent.

The basement is accessed by a long flight of stairs that is partially covered by a glass panel. This opening provides natural lighting for the office located in the basement, and accentuates the effect of inclusion of the kitchen volume in the ground floor.

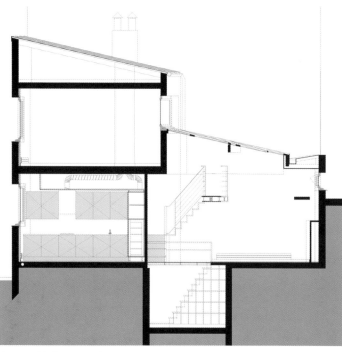

Across kitchen section

In the process of rehabilitating this building, the architects took into account all the aspects of its structure and its location in order to take full advantage of the natural lighting.

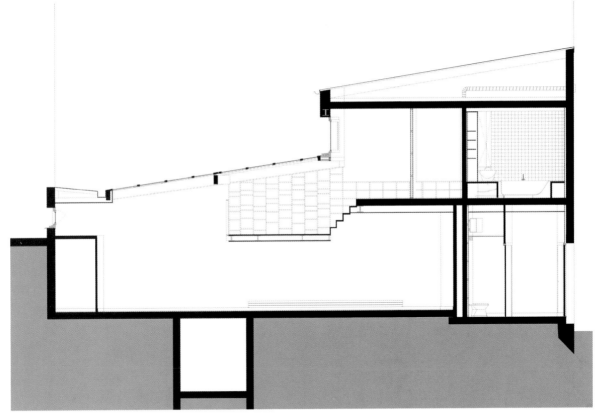

Across kitchen section

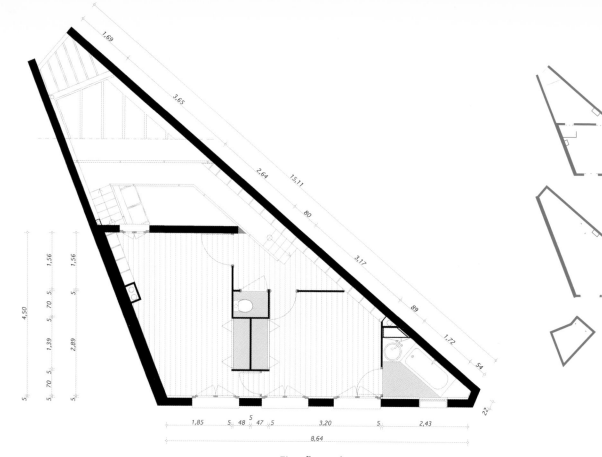

First floor plan

Basement plan

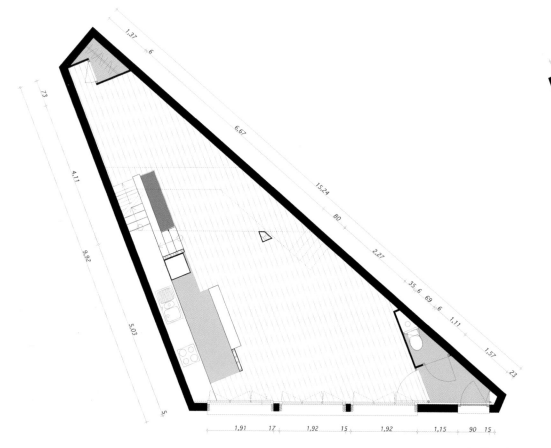

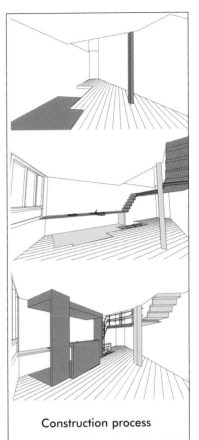

Construction process

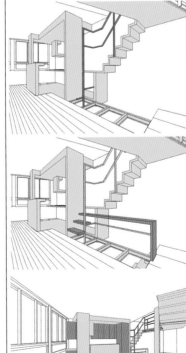

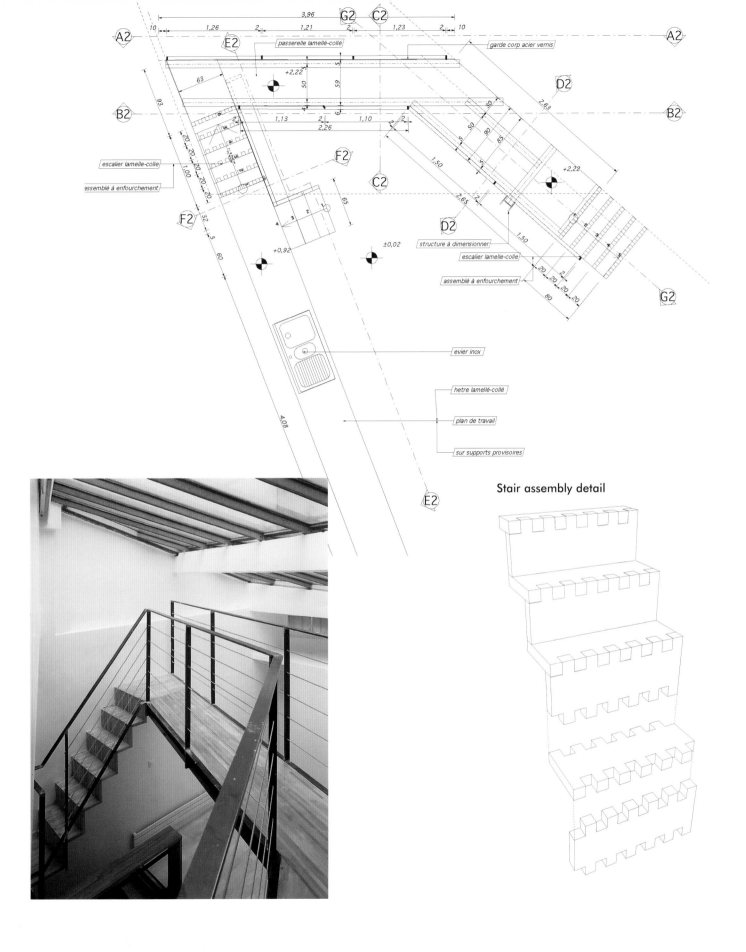

3,96

G2 C2

A2 A2

10 1,26 2 1,21 1,23 2 10

E2

passerelle lamellé-collé

garde corp acier vernis

D2

63 +2,22

50 59

B2 2,63 B2

escalier lamelle-collé

1,13 2 6 1,10

2,26

assemblé à enfourchement

F2

1,00

65

F2 32

5

60

structure à dimensionner

escalier lamelle-collé

assemblé à enfourchement

+0,92 ±0,02

D2

C2

50 90 85

1,50

2,65

1,50

+2,22

D2

G2

20 2 20 20

80

4,08

evier inox

hetre lamellé-collé

plan de travail

sur supports provisoires

E2

Stair assembly detail

111

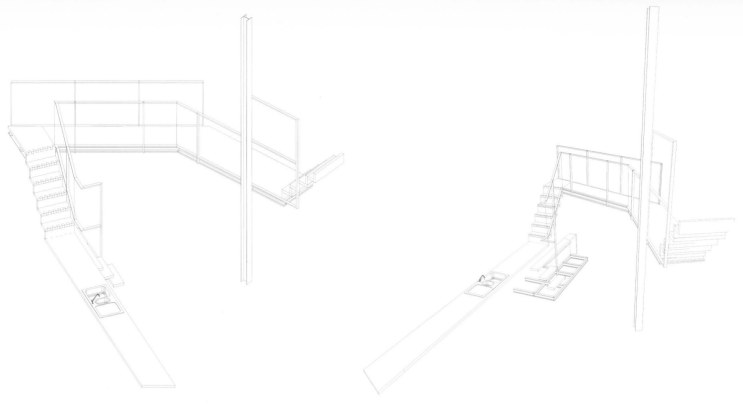

Axonometric views

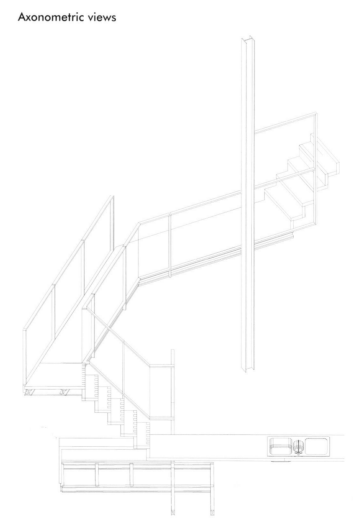

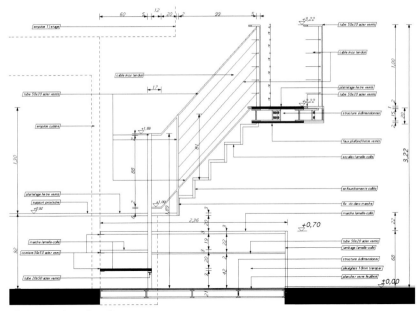

Construction details

The walkway —which serves as an access to the main room —maintains a continuity with the staircase and the kitchen module.

# Mónica Pla

## Guillermo's Loft

*Photographs:
José Luis Hausmann*

**Barcelona, Spain**

Before it was renovated, this old apartment located in Barcelona's Ciutat Vella quarter, featured a lot of rooms and little natural light. The deteriorated and neglected space has been transformed with the goal of creating a luminous and spacious residence in just one environment.

The first step was to tear down various walls and to open up -structure permitting- a number of windows to permit the entrance of natural light. With no walls left to divide the space, the designer managed to provide the bedroom with intimacy and to establish a difference between the kitchen and the living area. To separate the bedroom from the main room and still maintain spatial continuity, designer Monica Pla placed the bathroom between the two. Accessible from the bedroom, the bathroom contains a shower which is contained in a box with partial walls. The sink, mounted on one of the exterior faces of the box, is completely integrated into the bedroom space. The toilet is situated next to the entrance door and a sliding door completely isolates it from the central living area.

To obtain harmony in the apartment, the furnishings were carefully selected. On one of the lateral walls, a piece of IKEA furniture unites the entire space, from the kitchen-dining room to the living room. As a result, the kitchen is integrated with the living room, creating a warmer environment. In the living room, Pla exposed a brick wall and managed to define the room's independence by means of a sofa upholstered in brown canvas from DOM. The dining room table is from Pilma. The lighting, also from Pilma, contributes to the warmth of the space, as does the wooden floor.

By studying the placement of the pieces of furniture and other objects that make up the home, the interior designer achieved a functional and modern renovation that floods a remarkable, diaphanous space with light.

Light colors, used for the furnishings, the hardwood floors, and the kitchen cabinets, present a uniform and spacious atmosphere towards the hallway.

To incorporate the shower into the center of the space required the use of a piece of furniture to divide the apartment's two main areas. A small stair leads up to the shower and the new installations are hidden underneath this platform, which reinforces our perception of it as a foreign element placed on top of the original floor.

The first step in the renovation was the tearing down of all dividing walls to eliminate the profusion of tiny rooms and the opening up of as many windows as the structure would allow. In the living room, the original balcony doors were retained and restored and the masonry of one wall was exposed.

A shower has been placed in a newly-created volume that separates the bedroom from the living room, while maintaining visual continuity. This volume is slightly raised, with the necessary technical installations set beneath

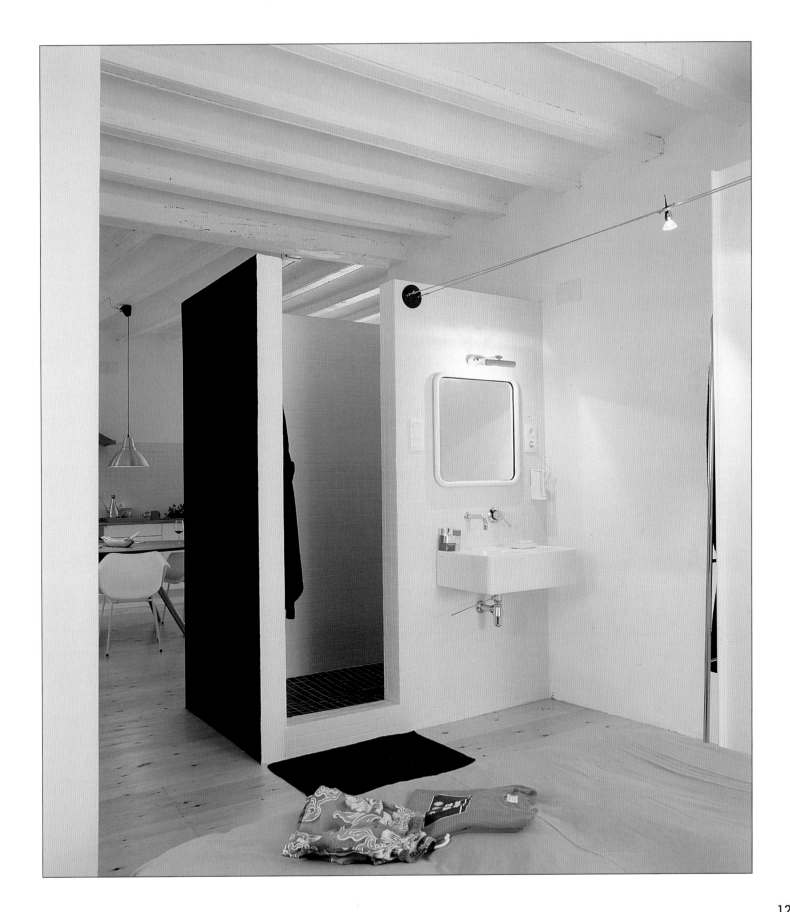

# Atelier Bow Wow

## Asama House

Photographs:
*Atelier Bow Wow*

**Kariuzawa, Japan**

This site is located on the edge of the famous mountain resort Karuizawa, 2 hours by car from Tokyo. Since it borders farm land, the area is a mixture of holiday homes and farm houses. To the west are rice paddies and to the east is forest. The project is a simple, single room for a family and is surrounded by 15-meter-high trees.

All the living spaces directly benefit from the daily shifts of natural light and views of the canopy of trees surrounding the home. The building is square in plan, with a pyramidal roof. The issue for this project was how to affect the purity of this form with the specific nature of the various orientations.

The ceiling space is divided into 5 portions by suspended walls giving a suggestion of rooms. The suspended walls act as large beams so that columns are not required, and a single space can be maintained below.

The position of the suspended walls is determined by the combination of proportions to suit activities such as dining, living, studying, sleeping and washing. The angles of the roof planes are also defined by these proportions.

The architects made every effort to incorporate the site's abundant light into the scheme. While the trunk-scape of the forest is framed, the tops of the trees with a backdrop of blue sky are pulled into the space by large openings. By planning the layout in this way, each of the 9 external surfaces of the house obtained an opening. The light qualities entering through each of these openings measure changing time, seasons and orientation. At sunset, a particular portion of the ceiling space becomes stained in a changing hue of orange, while the other portions show various shades of gray.

125

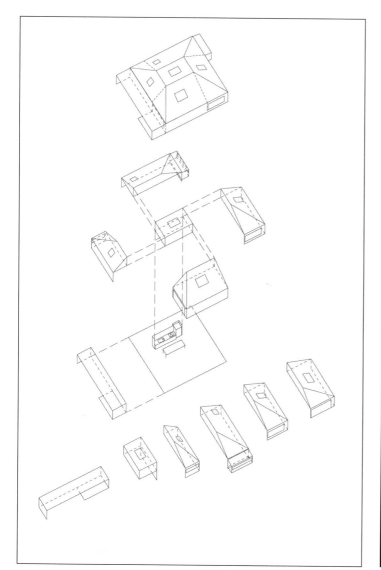

The design of the suspended walls eliminates the need for structural beams, while implying the division of the space below into "rooms".

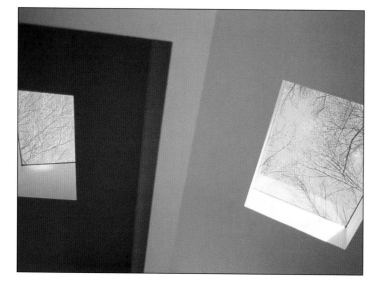

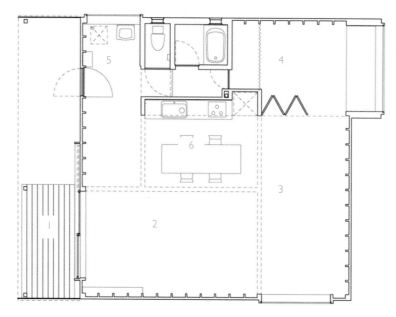

**Ground floor plan**

1. Terrace
2. Living room
3. Study
4. Bedroom
5. Lavatory
6. Dining room

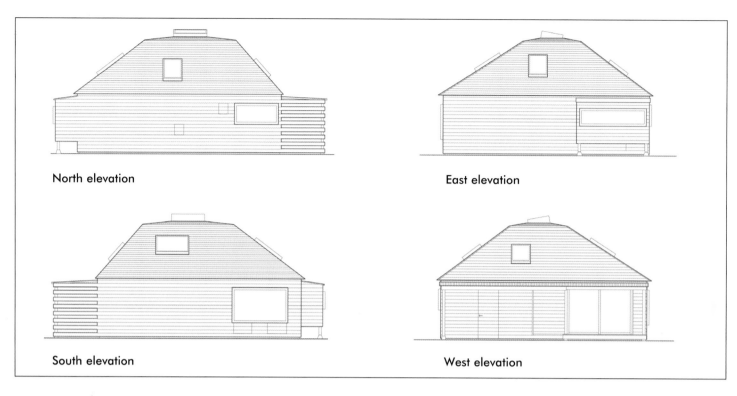

North elevation

East elevation

South elevation

West elevation

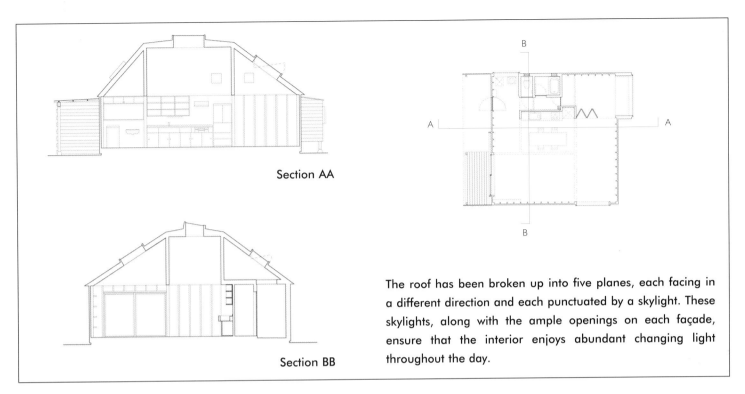

Section AA

Section BB

The roof has been broken up into five planes, each facing in a different direction and each punctuated by a skylight. These skylights, along with the ample openings on each façade, ensure that the interior enjoys abundant changing light throughout the day.

# ARCHITECTEN LAB

## Apartment V

Photographs:
*Phillipe Van Gelooven*

**Hasselt, Belgium**

The client's brief called for a clear-cut, minimal living space that would provide a comfortable environment with sufficient attention paid to ambience. Because of his busy lifestyle and subsequent desire to relax at home after a hard day's work, the owner preferred an uncluttered design which would also have enough space to enjoy the company of friends and family when entertaining.

Since the structure of the apartment building already largely dictated the interior spaces, which had been conceived as an open plan, the majority of the work took place in the kitchen. The final design was a simple rectangular beam which, when not in use, looks like a row of cupboards. It is constructed in a dark stained oak, in consonance with the dining table and the wooden floors.

The library wall and the fire place are designed to exercise a subdued presence in the room and to keep a low profile. This was achieved by making them the same color as the walls and keeping a restraint on the proliferation of details. Thus, it is the objects and books upon the shelves that focus the attention.

The same principle was used in the bedroom and the bathroom, where subdued colors are predominant, and the same materials are used as in the living area. Glass mosaic in the same color as the walls creates a spacious atmosphere in the shower and bathroom area.

In the bedroom, the headboard of the bed was made of the same oak as the flooring, once again ensuring a tranquil appearance and drawing attention to the bed itself and the artwork on the wall.

On the whole the design of this apartment tries to project an image of the owner's lifestyle and background, so he can feel at ease and relaxed in his home, surrounded by his personal belongings and the memories collected over the years, in a setting which is reserved and subdued, placing most of the focus on the inhabitant rather than on the interior itself.

Floor plan

The client requested a reserved and subdued space that would show a restraint of detail, a space that would grant him the freedom to make his own imprint on his surroundings. Dark oak flooring and shelving throughout the apartment provides a subtle, classic backdrop onto which the inhabitant can impose his own style at will.

The same guiding principle of subdued colors is evident in the bedroom and bathroom. In the bathroom, a glass mosaic motif adds the necessary tone of lightness and
visually opens the space.

# Anne Bugugnani

## LOFT 108

Photographs: Eugeni Pons

**Barcelona, Spain**

The first in a series, loft 1 was conceived as a 'prototype' compact loft dwelling, designed for a building made up of small workshops and a low-cost renovation budget.

The space enjoyed a great deal of natural light, which the architects made the most of by housing functional elements in low, transparent or perforated volumes. These were based on a single space-organizing module measuring 108cm.

The placement of the kitchen and bathroom facilities was resolved by compacting the two, to create more generous open spaces.

To encourage visual continuity, the range of colors used for the finishing materials was unified: white stucco, glass, and an unbroken floor over the existing cement slabs.

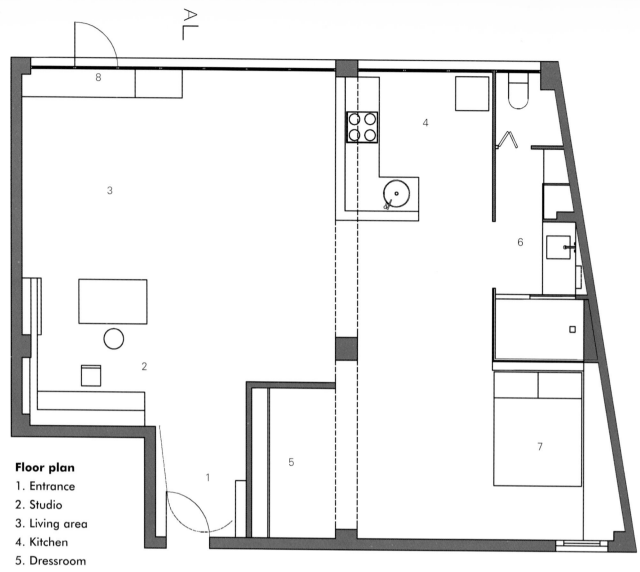

**Floor plan**

1. Entrance
2. Studio
3. Living area
4. Kitchen
5. Dressroom
6. Bathroom
7. Bedroom
8. Acces to terrace

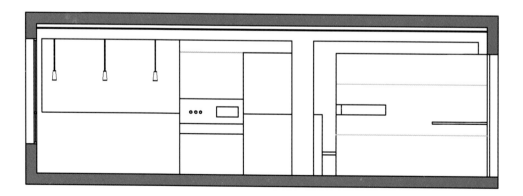

Section AA

To encourage visual continuity, the range of colors used for the finishing materials was unified: white stucco, glass, and an unbroken floor over the existing cement slabs.

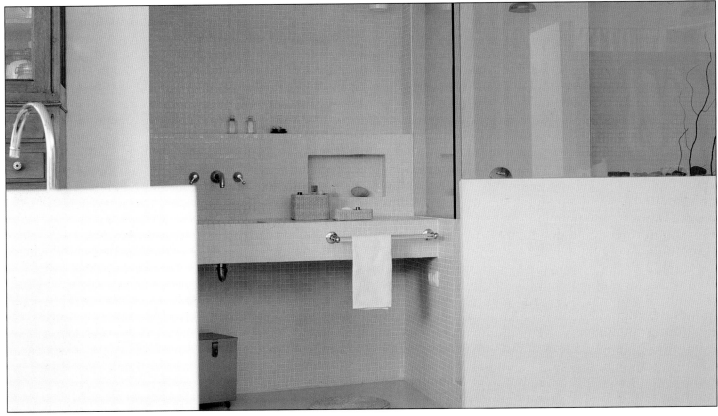

151

# Aase Kari Kvalvik

## Verven

Photographs: Nils Petter Dale

**Stavanger, Norway**

The scheme, is situated in Stavanger, Norway. The location is close to the city center, in between old seahouses, factory buldings and a large park and recreation area. This site offered a great possibility to develop a new, young, urban and social living concept.

The challenge was to combine old and new, changing a factory and industrial building into small dwelling units for young people, and at the same time preserving some of the buildings authenticity. Subdividing the wide and open space is a contradiction in it self. In a way, two opposite directions. The old buildings main character was perpendicular. The construction, the large ceiling heights, 3,5 m, the vertical windows in the facade, all together add equal a concept of vertical principle. Even when subdividing the wide open space into several small units, the verticality still exists.

The zoning plan gave an oppurtunity to build a new story on top of the old roof. The fourth story has an excellent height, 4,3 meters and also represents a vertical volume. Together with the existing structural elements in the facade the verticalness was achieved as a whole.

There is a balance between the original building and the modern elements both are evident after the reconstruction.

The main concept is based on creating small units which increased density in harmony with the existing qualities in the building. The scheme consists of 150 units. Each unit is based on the same model. Most of the units are 33 sqm, some are even less.

The ceiling height gave an oppurtunity to organize the units according to a simple principle: they should have as much natural daylight as possible and be spread outward addressing the open park.

The units primary organization is simple. One main wall is dividing the two different activities between quiet and active area. The bath has the same width as the bedroom. The access line was placed as a border line between the two different spaces.

The access line ends up in the front facade as a glass balcony. The facade and the balcony ensure a good spatial and visual connection between outside and inside.

The kitchen has been an important function when planning the units. By connecting the kitchen and the living room across the depth of the unit, the kitchen represents the entire unit. It has also been important to ensure enough space for baths. They are 4,5 sqm and include washing machines.

In contrast to the city´s vibrant and pulsating movement, the units represent a more calm and controlled environment within the urban fabric. The flexible small flats with their central location, make them ideal for young professionals just doing their first realestate investment. The units interact with a modern way of living where the boundaries of home and outside are more transparent. The city´s facilities like restaurants, bookshops and cafés becomes part of the living room.

# Roberto Silvestri

## A House in Piazza Navona

*Photographs: Ernesta Caviola*

**Rome, Italy**

Designing the interior spaces of a house allows you to work with emotions, to shape rooms that will hold inside feelings, angers, passions, moods. "The house is the life coffer," Le Corbusier used to say. Upon this concept we have based the project for the house of an italian film director; a house that had to gather the private world and the public life of the owner. A house that had to be, at the same time, "coffer" and "theatre" of life.

During the designing process, we have spent a long time together with the client talking about cinema, art, cooking, books, and being careful not to touch on technical problems. The idea was to create an interior space shaped exactly around the client's character and desires, without thinking too much about functional problems that, in this way, would have been naturally solved. For this reason, deep knowledge of the client has been so important; his ideas, his way of moving, his passions and tastes have been the functional program.

Working with these purposes, we managed to make a very sensitive place, a rich but not overwhelming space, a strong but warm and cozy place at the same time. We believe that it is impossible for mankind to live in geometrically perfect spaces, to stay in architecturally pure forms. For this reason, we have designed a rigorous house that speaks with feelings and the imperfections of human life. So the space is extremely open and fluent. The rooms are strictly connected, but at the same time, each single traditional room is still visible in the structure of the house. The house is not loft space, but is a real house divided into rooms that suit the contemporary way of Italian living.

The access to the house comes from above, walking on a three-step stair made of Travertino Navona slabs put on a light iron structure. The living room has very little furniture. The main character of the room is the front wall: dark, brown, velvety, non-homogeneous. This is the first of the two walls that are covered in Corten: rusted iron usually used in exteriors. This material is absolutely perfect for our purposes: it is warm, strong and capable of giving a beautiful atmosphere to the whole room. The two rusted walls form the space of the studio: a small, intimate and high tech place that can easily be transformed into another sleeping room.

The outside terrace is connected to the kitchen that is completely open to the rest of the house. In front of the kitchen, two openings in the ancient wall show the history of the place with its historical bricks made of Roman Tufo. This creates a strange contrast with the modern materials of the new project such as the aluminium wainscoting which is included within the wall itself.

The private spaces are very small: a bedroom and a bathroom. The first one has been designed around the client, so it is a very small place with just a bed and a wardrobe, both made of natural wood. Very different from this is the bathroom; a place for private luxury completely different from the rest of the house. The floor is made of big slabs of red marble that strongly contrast with the white of the walls that are partially covered with a very particular kind of tiles: the same tiles that the client saw in the Paris underground while he was starting an unforgettable love story.

Floor plan

A

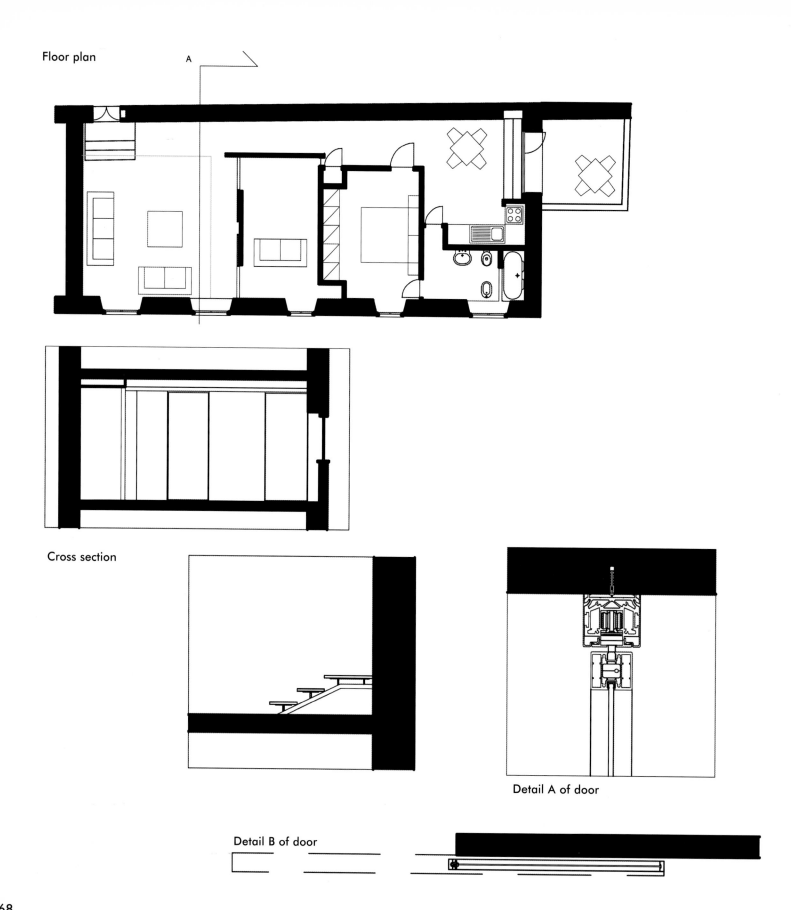

Cross section

Detail A of door

Detail B of door

# Jordi Galí

## Apartment in Barcelona

*Photographs: Jordi Miralles*

**Barcelona, Spain**

At the start of this project, the top slab of the pre-reform apartment was higher than it is now, the walls and flooring were greatly deteriorated and there were no dividing walls.

The program called for a single-occupant apartment, for which a diaphanous and unified space was created, installing dividing walls only in the bathroom.

Due to their visually degraded state, all of the perimetral walls were clad in Pladur up to the height of the beams of the slab, leaving a small portion of the top of the original walls bare. The five-centimeter space left between the Pladur and the original wall was put to use with the installation of indirect perimetral lighting throughout the apartment, thereby heightening the drama of the old wood beams and vaults. The entire kitchen volume, including the cupboards and shelves, were also done in Pladur. The cupboards were kept at a low height, the top part of the walls being clad in a Pladur partition which conceals the smoke extractor and a fireproof panel which, when lowered, hides the kitchen range and work area.

The paving was finished in cement dyed a greenish-gray. The sink is held up on the sides by transparent glass panels, visually tying it to the bedroom.

The bright light entering the interior of the dwelling is filtered by a venetian blind system.

# 5th Studio

## Eden Street / Clarendon Street

Photographs:
David Grandorge

Cambridge, UK

The House in the Garden of Eden was built in the mid-1800s in a former area of land known as the Garden of Eden. The project appeared at first to be concerned with the improvement of the existing single storey kitchen with bathroom beyond. As an initial investigation, the architects drew up a long term plan for moving the bathroom upstairs, the kitchen into the centre of the house and the main bedroom into a position in the garden. The client's tight budget dictated that the architects needed to institute an initial phase of work to make the house habitable and safe. The property was very poorly built and the former owner had removed the staircase.

Set perpendicularly to the former stair, which rose from the lower level of the back room to renegotiate three awkward split-levels towards the front of the house, the new stair begins in the front room and replaces much of the central division of the house. An intermediate landing formed in glass gives onto the flying-freehold room, and the future bathroom at the back of the house. A further flight rises to the front bedroom, reappearing in the front room below like a puzzle. The elision of the central structure of the house allows a top lit double height space to be formed that lights the middle of the house and emphasises the tripartite cellular and private character of "upstairs" as against the free-flowing levels of downstairs.

The Clarendon Street Project is the partial rehabilitation of a fairly typical mid-terrace Victorian house in central Cambridge. The clients had undergone an earlier remodelling of the space of the original house in the mid-1970s, but a cold and leaking back extension provided the opportunity to form a new sort of space between the house and the garden.

The existing single storey room had been built between the garden walls of the terrace. Its flat roof was leaking, and the single glazed softwood screen that formed the rear elevation at ground floor was in a poor state. The space was dark and cold.

The room mediates between the spaces of house and garden. The new space lies at the end of a ground floor plan that is bisected along the centre of the house into a kitchen and a library. Both of these twin avenues into the room are dark; the reworked space of the room is highly lit in contrast by a glass roof over half the room, and by a floor to ceiling glazed screen to the garden.The luminous quality of the garden room emphasises and makes positive the relative darkness of the library and kitchen.

The room itself is treated as two halves: the kitchen side is wholly top-lit, while the library side has a plastered soffit.

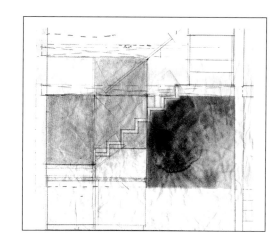

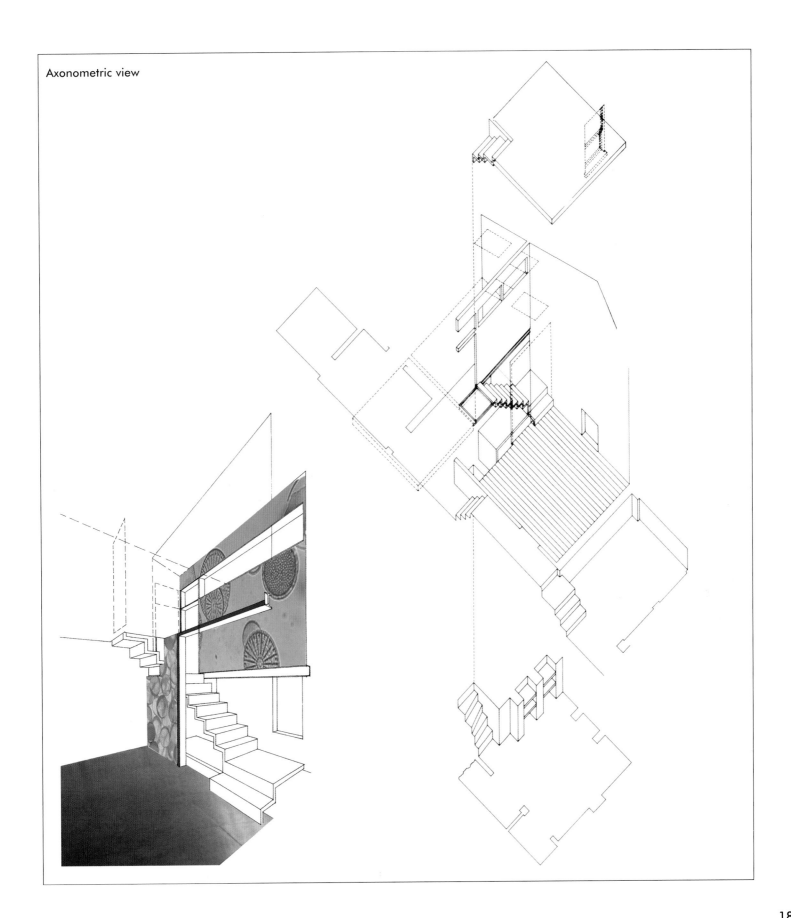

Axonometric view

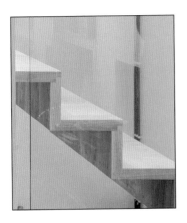
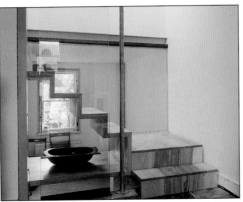
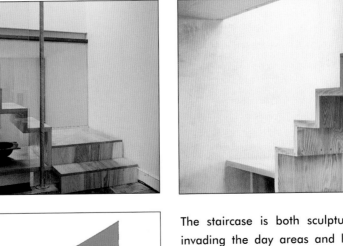

The staircase is both sculptural and functional, invading the day areas and linking the different environments of the dwelling. It is not a typical vertical circulation space but an essential element in the distribution of the scheme.

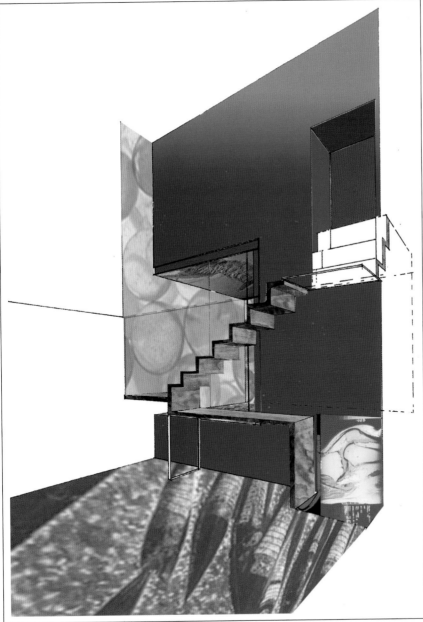

189

The large glazed door that separate the kitchen and the library from the garden act like a picture frame. Thus, the garden penetrates the interior of the dwelling and brings coolness and greenery into the domestic environment.

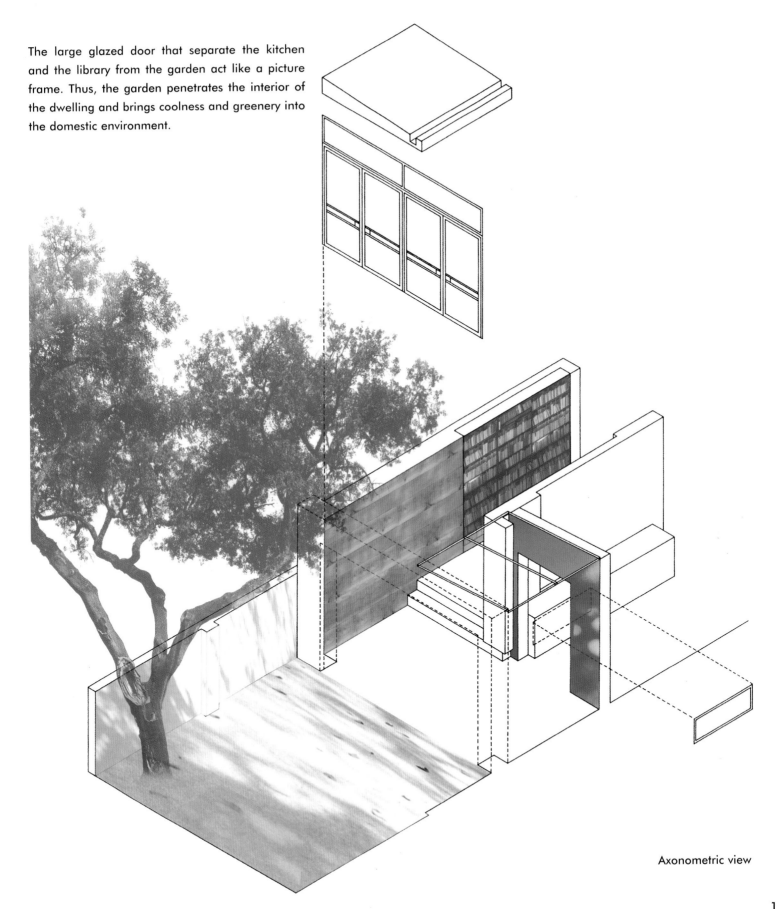

Axonometric view

The careful selection of materials used in the rehabilitation allowed the extension to be integrated into both the garden and the house, acting as a transition space between interior and exterior and providing originally dark rooms with good natural lighting.

# Mark Guard

## Apartment in Bankside Lofts

*Photographs: Henry Wilson*

London, UK

This apartment presented several problems. The client requirement for two bedrooms, as well as the desire to maximise the living area, was complicated by the relatively low ceiling heights. The only means of providing a satisfactory double-height space was by combining the sleeping platforms with another function.

The master bedroom therefore sits above the dressing area, accessed through a large pivoting door. The guest bedroom, adjacent the main entrance, is atop the guest bathroom. The circular stainless steel shower extends into the main living area and provides a sculptural counterpart to the more geometric forms of the master bedroom, with its "Z" shaped bed head. A stone clad staircase provides the route up to the guest sleeping platform, maximising the floor space in the main living area.

The split-level stone bathroom is positioned halfway between the dressing room and the master bedroom above. To allow light from the window in the bathroom to serve both the bedroom and the bathroom; the latter is open plan. However, as the bathroom is on a lower level, it is not visible from the bedroom, and so the perception of space in the bedroom is maximised.

The WC is placed in a circular etched glass-topped enclosure next to the steps leading up to the bathroom. Sliding the curved door automatically activates the lighting and ventilation system.

The floor of the bathroom is like a small landscape, with variyng levels and forms. The limestone floor, which is electrically heated, steps up to the bathroom and then down to form the bath-shower. A purpose-designed polished stainless steel swimming pool ladder provides a secondary means of access to the bathroom from the bedroom.

A large sliding canvas screen can be drawn across the main space, effectively sealing the master bed area from the living space. The apartment was designed to adapt easily to forthcoming developments in entertaining technology. A compartment has been let into the suspended ceiling in order to take a television projection unit, which will display on the large 5x3 m sliding screen. In the master bed area, a space has been designated for a flat screen television, enabling new technology to be seamlessly integrated into the apartment with minimum disruption. A concrete pillar, part of the building's original structure, has been left untouched in the main living area.

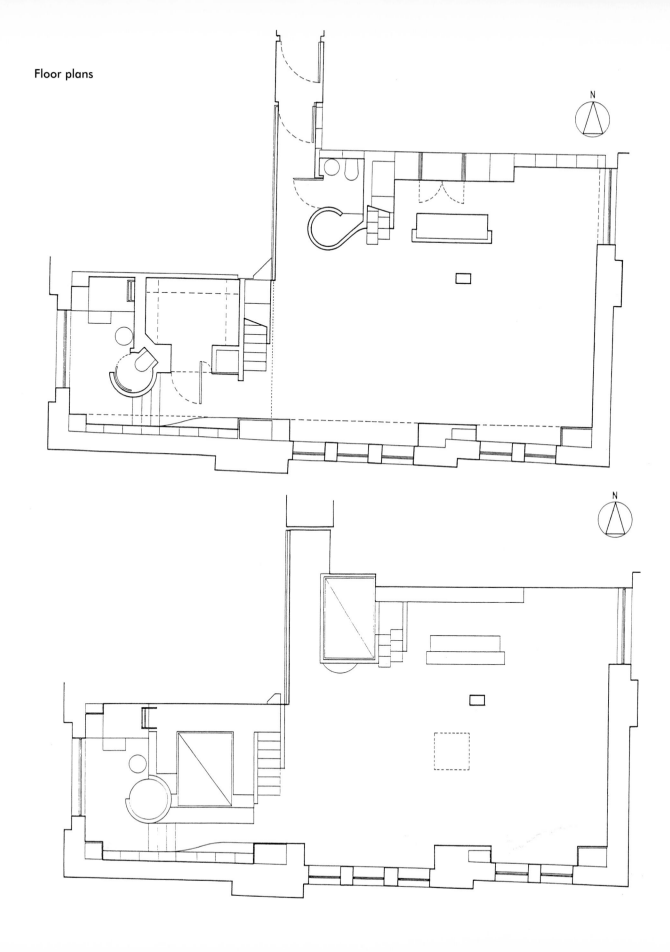

Floor plans

The kitchen is set behind a free.-standing counter with a tough-ened glass strorage shelf. This counter contains the oven, hob, preparation surfaces and waste.

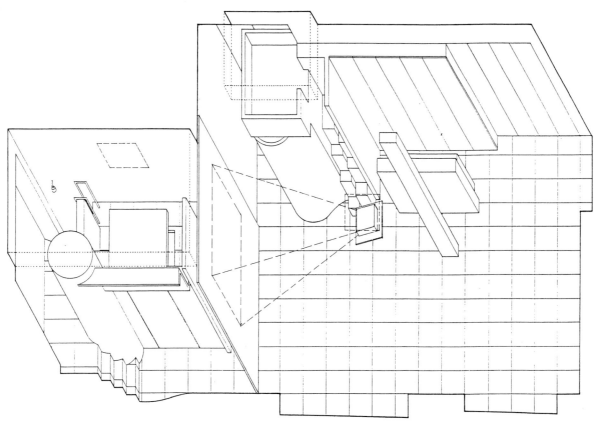

Axonometric view ground floor plan with proyector

Ground floor plan

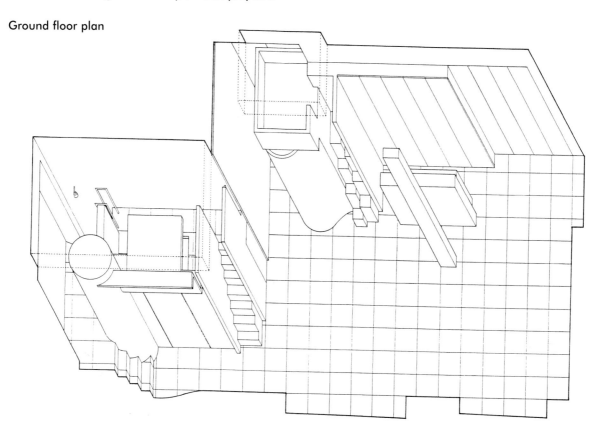

The bright primary colours chosen for the furniture contrast with
the white finishes and give the environment a dynamic quality.

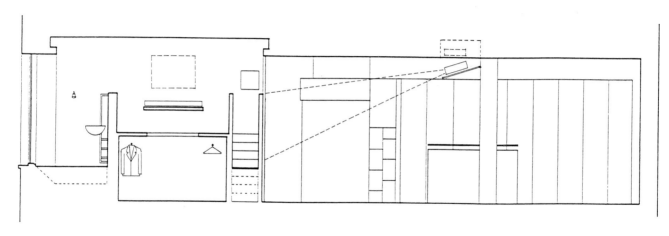

Section

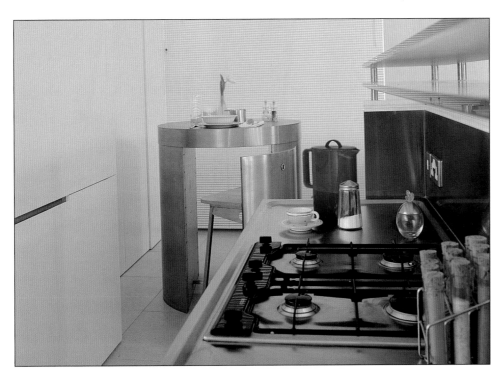

A circular stainless steel washbasin is attached to the wall of the raised bedroom. The mirror above the washbasin can be adjusted to a number of positions, and conceals a small bathroom cabinet.

# José Gigante

## Wind Mill Reconverting

Photographs:
*Luís Ferreira Alves*

**Vilar de Mouros,
Caminha, Portugal**

In the grounds of a recovered house in northern Portugal, an old abandoned windmill waited its turn to be useful again. In the course of time the idea finally arose of transforming this peculiar building into a small auxiliary dwelling belonging to the main house, giving it its own life and thus creating a completely inhabitable and independent space that could be used as a place of rest. For José Gigante, the architect in charge of the conversion, the presence of the mill was so strong that any major intervention would have minimised its charm. Therefore, without touching any of the thick granite walls, an unusual cooper roof with a very gentle slope was added. The intention was to respect the memory of the place as far as possible, so the inspiration for the transformation began naturally from the inside towards the outside. The layout and organisation of the small space, with only eight square metres per floor, was not easy. Thanks to the choice of wood as the main building material, a welcoming atmosphere enhanced by the curved walls and the few openings was achieved. On the lower floor, an impressive rock acts as an entrance step. On this level it was attempted to achieve a minimum space in which it was possible to carry out different activities. It houses a bathroom and a living room, with the possibility of transforming a small sofa into a curious bed: it is conceived as a case that contains all the necessary pieces for assembling the bed. On the upper floor, the furnishings are limited to a cupboard and a table/bed that is extended to the window.

The only openings are those that already existed in the mill and they have been left as they were conceived, with their natural capacity to reveal the exterior and to illuminate a space in which the contrasts between the materials cannot be ignored. The typology of this building was crucial to the restorations to which it has been subjected, and shows why the interior space is so important in this scheme. The thick circular walls occupy more space than the interior of the mill, but they hug the whole room and provide a welcoming and unconventional sensation that give this building a new and innovative perspective.

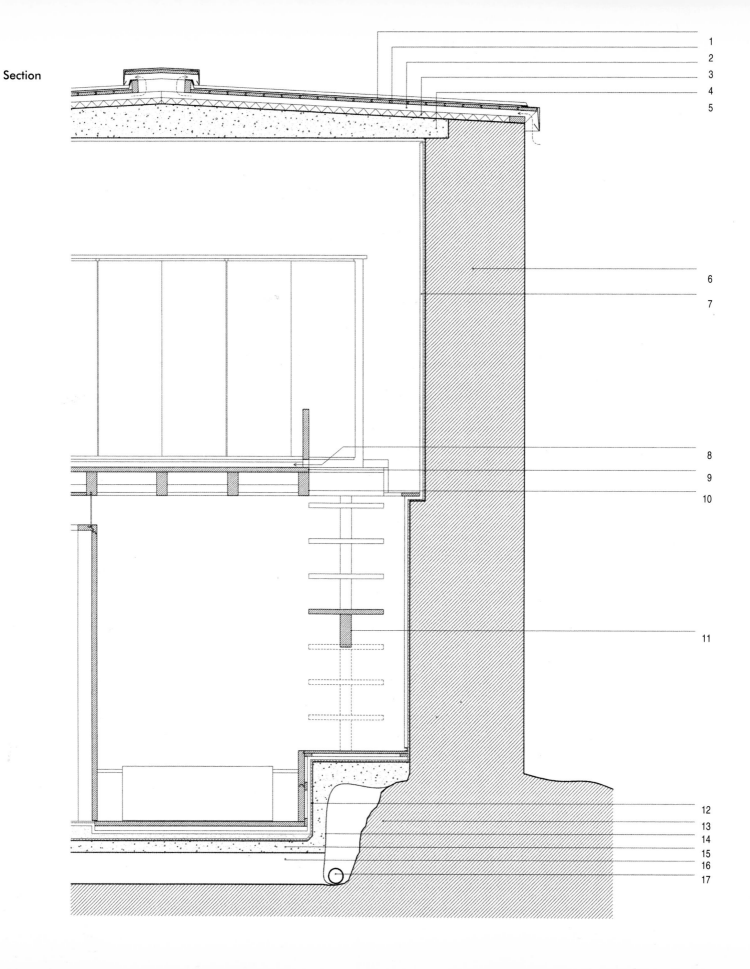

1
2
3
4
5

6

7

8

9

10

11

12
13
14
15
16
17

1. Copper cladding
2. Pine platform
3. Air chamber
4. Thermal insulation
5. Reinforced concrete panel
6. Existing granite masonry
7. Render
8. Air chamber
9. Beech wood floor
10. Beech wood frame
11. Beech wood staircase
12. Waterproof mortar
13. Existing rocky dike
14. Geotextile
15. Concrete wall
16. Gravel box
17. Pipe

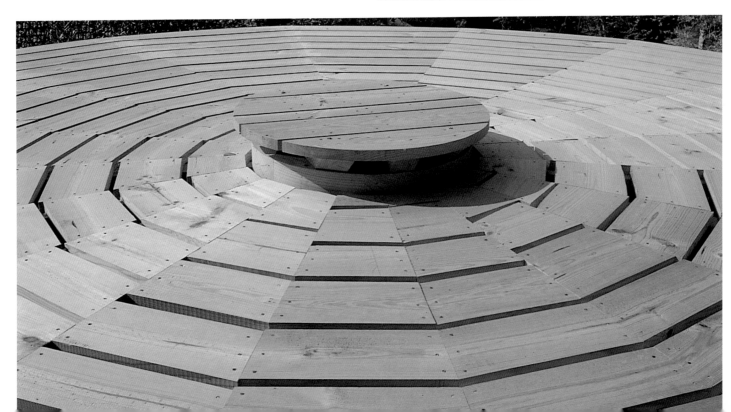

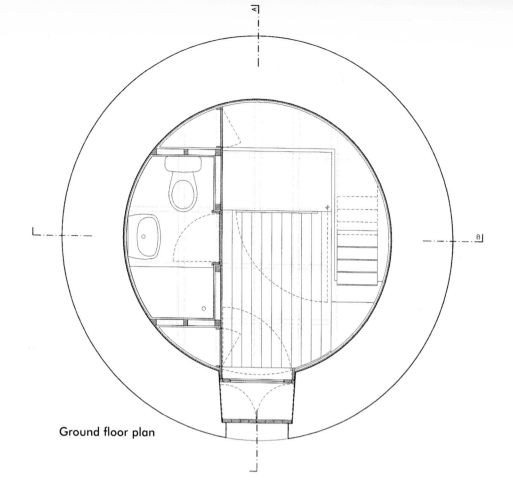

Ground floor plan

Upper floor plan

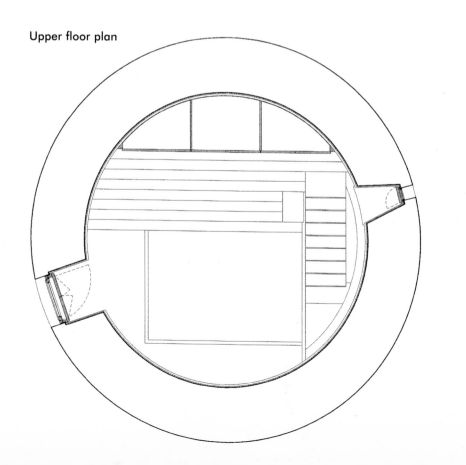

The choice of wood as the main construction element in the rehabilitation, in perfect combination with the white curved walls, creates a calm and welcoming atmosphere.

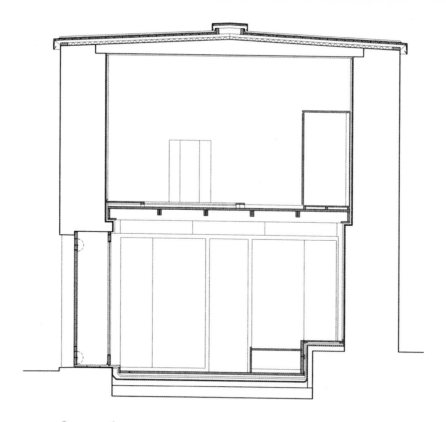

Cross sections

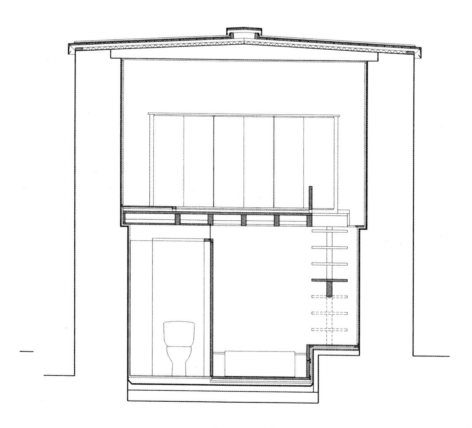

The use of wood and the maximum use of space are the main characteristics of this scheme. To solve the problem of the lack of space, a system was devised in which a bed is hidden at the foot of the staircase.

# Estudio Farini Bresnick

## Renovation of an apartment

*Photographs: Silvio Posada*

**Madrid, Spain**

The rehaul of this apartment in a 1970s building near Madrid's Plaza Mayor was an attempt to make maximum use of a reduced space. The original distribution was anodyne, a sort of apart-hotel, with a bedroom, bathroom and living room, and a kitchen built into a cupboard. Doors opening onto two balconies provide the only sources of natural light.

The program sought out the spatial connection and articulation of each function. The functions have been left in place, yet the connections and relationships between them have been modified. A module bringing together closet, dressing room, office and bathroom into a single piece is the unifying element.

In order to save space and define separate volumes, all doors are sliding panels. The bedroom and sitting room are connected via a wide opening that can be closed off with a sliding door, which thus serves as a partition wall as well. This sliding action shuts off the bedroom/living room connection, while at the same time revealing a work station built into the newly laid-out module. The other side of this module is a small closet in the entryway, next to the bathroom. A thin partition closes off the sides of the tall kitchen fixtures, a detail that reinforces the mini-space of the entryway.

As a fundamental aspect of the spatial definition, the apartment has been conceived in its furnished state. Thus, the study table and shelf have been set back into the module, and the dining room table has been specifically chosen and placed to subdivide the living room into distinct zones.

White dominates on the walls and doors. The work station and dining room table are in oak, to match the parquet flooring. The kitchen is deliberately abstract, with built-in appliances for a clean, unobstructed look. The countertop is of white imitation stone; the bathroom has been finished in bluish-gray stoneware tiles measuring 10x10 cm, with a white marble countertop. A cabinet behind the mirror has ample space for a number of items.

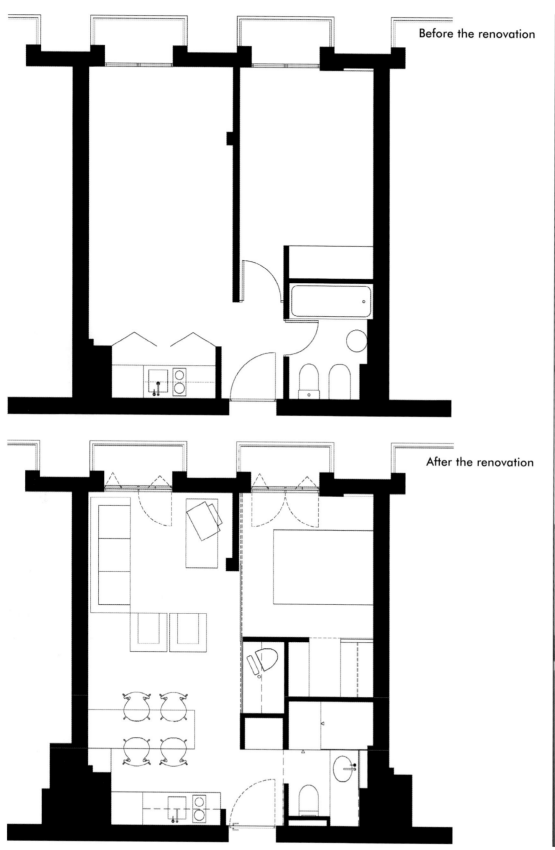

Before the renovation

After the renovation

216

The bedroom and sitting room are connected via a wide opening that can be closed off with a sliding door, which thus serves as a partition wall as well. This sliding action shuts off the bedroom/living room connection, while at the same time revealing a work station built into the newly laid-out module.

# Drewes Architects

## Cordes Apartment

Photographs:
Christian Richters

**Herzebrock-Clarholz,
Germany**

This complete remodeling of a conventionally laid out attic apartment grew from the client's wish for a loft-like living space. The removal of all possible dividing walls and partitions contributed to an open, continuous impression, but the centrally located staircase and bathroom present a barrier to a completely unitary visualization of the different areas. Yet at the same time, these basically disruptive elements are helpful as an organizing fulcrum around which the different functions of the loft can be grouped. As a result there is an open flow of space from the living area through the kitchen into the sleeping and bathing complex.

Eliminating the ceiling above the living and dining areas created generous vertical space and produced the option of the study gallery on the upper level which is accessible by means of a minimalist steel stairway. The kitchen is the core of the loft and is a hinge between the living and sleeping areas, with the countertop protruding into the living space in order to increase the spatial interconnections.

Visual connections and axes exist diagonally from the kitchen up to the bed and from the grand piano to the bathtub at the opposite end of the loft. The sleeping and bathing area is thus fully integrated into the open living space and is experienced as such by visitors entering the loft. For privacy, a massive sliding door of solid oak can separate the sleeping area.

A seamless floor of self-leveling epoxy, trowelled walls, steel, precast concrete and solid waxed oak reflect a simplicity and honesty reminiscent of the clients southern Italian heritage. The architecture takes a quiet and distant stand - a delicately differentiated background - liberating the space for the client's daily activities.

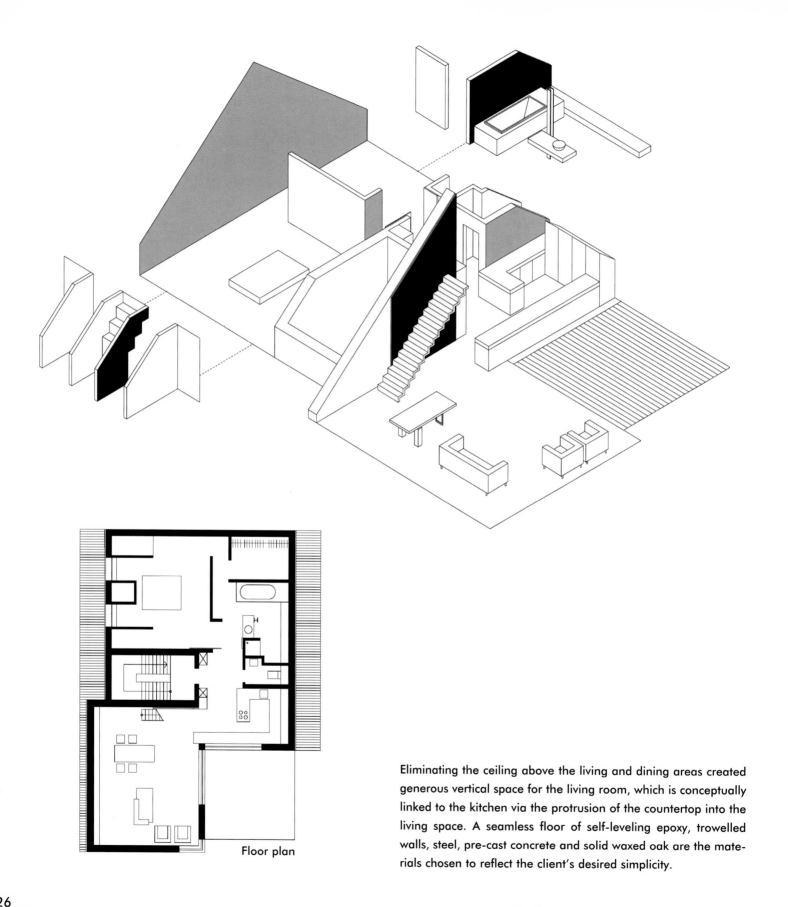

Floor plan

Eliminating the ceiling above the living and dining areas created generous vertical space for the living room, which is conceptually linked to the kitchen via the protrusion of the countertop into the living space. A seamless floor of self-leveling epoxy, trowelled walls, steel, pre-cast concrete and solid waxed oak are the materials chosen to reflect the client's desired simplicity.

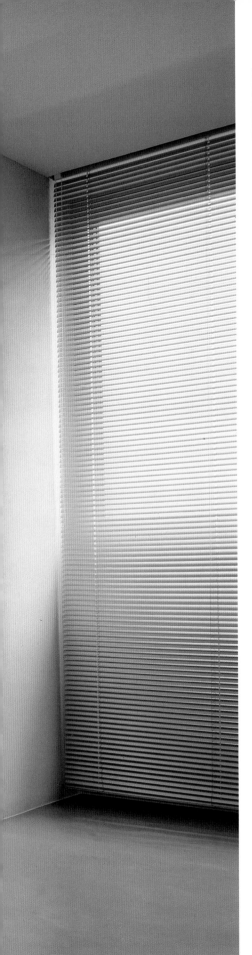

# Fabienne Couvert & Guillaume Terver

## Villa les Roses

Photographs:
Contributed by the architects

**Aix-en-Provence,
France**

This dwelling, built in the fifties, is an inhabitable pavilion of 60 sqm located at the entrance to a forest in the north-west of Aix-en-Provence that has been declared a protected area. As the regulations of the area only permitted the construction of 30% of the plot, the old garage had to be rehabilitated and enlarged to respond to the new needs of the clients, a couple with two children.

The dwelling has a living room, kitchen, bathroom, scullery, office and two bedrooms. This scheme thus responds to two seemingly contradictory requirements: to allow each room to work independently without this being a nuisance, and to maintain a large fluidity between the spaces.

The distribution of the functional programme is governed by two perpendicular elements that allow the space to be occupied. The first element consists of a technical block housing the kitchen, the scullery, a toilet and a bathroom. The second element is formed by a functional block housing the cupboards, a mobile partition and an office. The doors and woodwork were made in okume plywood.

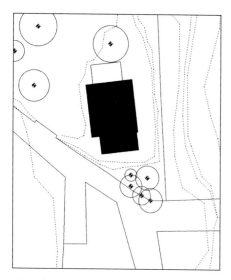

Site plan

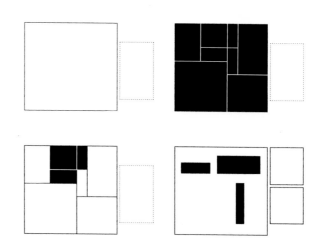

The use of mobile elements such as the wooden panels that connect or isolate the kitchen from the dining/living room provides total flexibility and versatility in the use of the space, creating atmospheres that adapt easily to the most immediate necessities of the occupants.

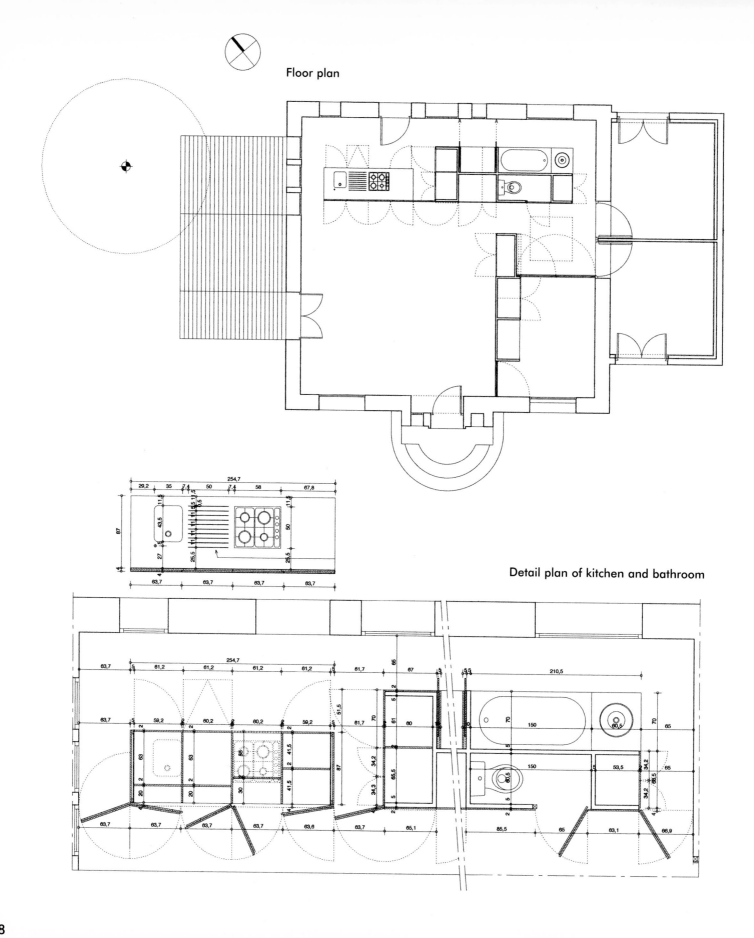

Floor plan

Detail plan of kitchen and bathroom

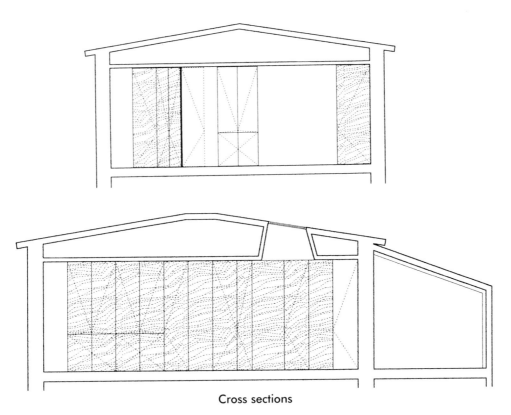

Cross sections